2.98

# Covered Bridges

## *OF THE MIDDLE ATLANTIC STATES*

THE COLOSSUS, AT PHILADELPHIA

# Covered Bridges

*OF THE*

*MIDDLE ATLANTIC*
*STATES*

BY

RICHARD SANDERS ALLEN

BONANZA BOOKS · NEW YORK

## ILLUSTRATION CREDITS

The author is grateful to E. H. Royce of St. Albans, Vermont, for his end paper photograph; to the Yale University Art Gallery for permission to use as a frontispiece the Arkell aquatint of The Colossus, and to Lambert Photos for the Uhlertown, Pennsylvania, canal bridge opposite the Table of Contents. Illustrations not otherwise noted below are from the author's own collection. For the rest, thanks are due (*reading left to right across the page, and then down*) to: p. 2—Harold F. Eastman, Thomas Paine Historical Association; p. 4—Historical Society of Pennsylvania, George B. Pease Coll.; p. 8—Pennsylvania Historical and Museum Commission; p. 10—Pennsylvania Power & Light Company; p. 12—Mrs. John Alden Chapman for her gift of the wash drawing by William Ladd Taylor; p. 13—H. B. Nields Coll.; p. 14—Mrs. Ruth S. Bliss; p. 23—Railway & Locomotive Historical Society; p. 25—(portrait) Erie Railroad; p. 28—Harold F. Eastman; p. 31—Lucy G. Loekle; p. 36—National Archives; p. 42—(top) Rolph Townshend; p. 43—two from Delaware Highway Department; p. 45—*Baltimore Sun,* Frank H. Jacobs; p.46—C. I. Ways, New York Herald Tribune, Inc.; p. 47—Peale Museum; p. 49—(left row down) John W. Poteet, Jr., (right row) Caroline Sprague, Lucy G. Loekle; p. 53—(bottom) William C. Witte; p. 54—(top two) J. A. Jacobs, (plan and bottom) David G. Williams; p. 56—(four left) Chris. W. Viehl, (two right) Walter W. Pryse; p. 58—(three lower) Walter W. Pryse; p. 59—(two) Chris. W. Viehl; p. 60—Chris. W. Viehl, (two) Walter W. Pryse; p. 62—John L. Warner, (lower three) Will G. Brown; p. 66—Mrs. J. R. Doty, George R. Wills; p. 68—George R. Wills; p. 70—George R. Wills; p. 71—three from Chris. W. Viehl; p. 72—J. Richard Gaintner, George R. Wills; p: 73—H. Warren Groff; p. 74—(top spread) the late Arthur L. Riemann, John J. Brindley, Harold Sitler; p. 77—H. Warren Groff; p. 78—(bottom) H. Warren Groff; p. 79—two from Ford Motor Company; p. 81—Roy Brooks, E. W. Plimpton, Virginia Highway Department, E. W. Plimpton, Lucy G. Loekle; p. 82—Caroline Sprague, Lucy G. Loekle, Virginia Highway Department; pp. 83, 84 and 85—Virginia Highway Department; p. 88—American Society of Civil Engineers; p. 89—Mrs. Janey Chenoweth Harris; p. 90—(Sink's Mill, Indian Creek) Lucy G. Loekle, (Wadestown) Roger D. Griffin, balance from H. B. Nields Coll.; p. 91—West Virginia Highway Department; p. 93—National Archives; p. 94—Columbia Historical Society, National Archives; p. 95—National Park Service; p. 96—(top) H. B. Nields Coll.; p. 98—NEA Service; p. 99—Atlantic Refining Company; p. 101—two from George R. Wills; p. 102—(bottom) McNaught Syndicate, Inc.; p. 103—J. K. Rathmell, Wide World Photos; p. 104—George R. Wills, Thomas McNamara, John W. Poteet, Jr., Richard Bullock. The jacket photograph, by the author, is of the Twin Bridges near Forks, Pennsylvania.

TO DORIS
WHOSE LOVE, GENTLE PERSUASION AND
INSTINCTIVE GOOD SENSE KEPT ME FROM
THE PATHS OF PROCRASTINATION

## ACKNOWLEDGMENTS

As in COVERED BRIDGES OF THE NORTHEAST, a great number of people helped make this book. George Daly drew the sketches, maps and diagrams which illustrate the text. The archives of the various historical societies were a prime source, among them:

The Historical Society of Pennsylvania, Philadelphia.
Pennsylvania Historical and Museum Commission, Harrisburg.
Historical Society of Western Pennsylvania, Pittsburgh.
The Maryland Historical Society, Baltimore.
The Public Archives Commission, Dover, Delaware.

Many, many state, county and local historical societies, highway departments and officials, civic groups and history-minded individuals contributed information. Fellow hobbyists unstintingly gave of their time and the results of their personal researches, among them:

PENNSYLVANIANS
Mrs. Ruth S. Bliss
John J. Brindley
Mrs. John R. Brown
Mrs. J. R. Doty
Henry C. Falk
Edward J. Fisher*
Earle R. Forrest
Roy R. Fuller
J. Richard Gaintner
H. Warren Groff
George M. Hart
Mrs. Vernon Hoffman
Miss Eleanor G. King
H. W. Laubenstein
Mrs. Elsie Singmaster Lewars*
Mr. and Mrs. Thomas
  McNamara
G. S. Michener
Mrs. M. LeRoy Moyer
Walter W. Pryse
Mrs. Gordon Rainey
Arthur L. Riemann
Mrs. Thomas Schade
William H. Stephens
Mrs. Ellanor M. Thomas
Cornelius Weygandt*
David G. Williams
George R. Wills

DELAWAREANS
Nathaniel D. Rand
David K. Witheford

MARYLANDERS
Mr. and Mrs. John W. Poteet, Jr.
H. Grattan K. Tyrrell

WASHINGTONIANS
Mrs. Frank Stolzenbach
Robert M. Vogel

VIRGINIANS
J. D. Capron
Lee H. Nelson

WEST VIRGINIANS
Calvin R. Conaway
Dr. E. E. Myers
Herbert B. Nields*
C. A. Rothrock
Mrs. Delbert Squires

NEW ENGLANDERS
Laurence Beake
Michael DeVito
Mrs. Byron Dexter
Mr. and Mrs. Harold F. Eastman
Mrs. Herbert G. Foster

Mrs. Hiram R. Gatchell
Miss Charlotte P. Goddard
Roger D. Griffin
Mrs. Dorothy P. Harvey*
Mr. and Mrs. Orrin H. Lincoln
Leo Litwin
Miss Rae Osborn
George B. Pease
J. M. Puffer
William Schermerhorn
Mrs. Charles Hadley Watkins

NEW YORKERS
Dann Chamberlin
Fred Eidenbenz
Dr. G. L. Howe
Mrs. W. H. Lough
William D. Mohr
William D. Owen
John L. Warner
Harley A. Williams*
Joseph H. Wilson
Frederick C. Wunsch

JERSEYITES
Mrs. Albert Day
Mrs. Lucy G. Kemp
Harry B. Tryon

*Deceased

ESPECIAL THANKS are extended to Dolly and Harold Sitler of Hershey, Pennsylvania, and James K. Rathmell, Jr., of Lansdale, Pennsylvania, whose personal knowledge and generosity made the Pennsylvania census reasonably complete. Also to Ladislav Dejnozka for his timely aid in photographic work, and most of all to Janet Greene for many pertinent suggestions and untold hours of editing to make things hang together.   R. S. A.

# CONTENTS

## But Why Covered?

"Keeps 'em dry," an old Pennsylvania carpenter always answered. Not the travelers, not the horses, or the wagonloads of hay, or the sweethearts halted in the fragrant shadows; nor was he referring to the plank roadways of the old landmarks. The roofs were put on our old covered bridges to keep the great main beams and arches dry. Staunch as these supporting timbers are, they rot if left exposed to be alternately wet by rains and snow and then scorched by sun.

Builders in Maryland and the Virginias put the facts less bluntly but they felt the same way about it.

"Our bridges were covered, my dear Sir, for the same reason that our belles wore hoop skirts and crinolines—to protect the structural beauty that is seldom seen, but nevertheless appreciated."

# America's First Covered Bridge

THE BRIEF ceremonies were over and the late afternoon sun slanted warmly into the fresh excavation on the riverbank. In the pit a lanky stonemason, John Lewis, gave a final whack with mallet and chisel to the medium-sized granite block at his feet. Then he dusted his gnarled hands and stood

In a way, John Lewis' faith has been justified, for to the best of anyone's knowledge his handiwork is still buried deep, waiting for people more learned to unearth it. It lies beneath the silt, ashes and grit of nearly a hundred and sixty years of traffic, forming part of the eastern abutment of Philadelphia's present-day Mar-

Schuylkill Permanent Bridge.

back to admire his inscription, cut deep in the rugged gray stone:

TFCSOTSPBWL OCTOBER XVIII MDCCC

"Say, John," an idler hailed from the bank above. "Who's to tell what them letters mean, when they dig it up?"

Lewis looked up toward the voice and then back at his lettering. He knew he should have carved out the full legend, but there just hadn't been room.

"Why, sir," he replied courteously, "by the time they dig up this here stone, the people will be much more learned than you and I be!"

With that the mason picked up his tools and went home, making his way through the waist-high brown grass in the fields along the wide and beautiful river.

ket Street Bridge across the Schuylkill River. If or when it does come to light, perhaps the finders will be learned enough to decipher its meaning:

THIS FIRST CORNER STONE OF
THE SCHUYLKILL PERMANENT BRIDGE
WAS LAID OCTOBER 18, 1800

Thus did mason John Lewis mark the start of America's first covered bridge. Not only would it become the pride of Philadelphia, but it would serve as the prototype for thousands of spans which played their large part in expanding the young United States.

Luckily for researchers, so great and wondrous a project as crossing the Schuylkill with a permanent bridge—ferries and a lurching pontoon affair had done unsteady service for

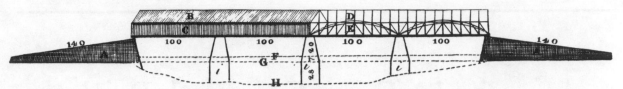

*First published U. S. covered bridge design, from the* Columbian Magazine *of January, 1787. A A represent abutments; B is roof on half the bridge; D is the other half, uncovered to show rafters; C is weatherboarding; E shows truss work and method of framing without weatherboards; F & G are high- and low-water marks; H shows riverbed.*

years—prompted much comment and many plans. The first appeared in 1787, when the *Columbian Magazine* offered a "suggested design" by which an anonymous draftsman proposed to bridge the river at High (now Market) Street. His idea called for four spans, each a hundred feet long, whose arches would rest on piers and abutments and would carry a flat roadway—and his bridge was to be *covered!* Concerning the unusual addition of a roof to his structure, the author said not a word. The meager descriptive text and illustration form the earliest known published reference to an American covered bridge.

Who was responsible for the *Columbian* article? No one knows. But it could have been Thomas Paine, the Revolutionary spark plug and political writer: he was a bridge enthusiast, and he was visiting Philadelphia in time to have masterminded the story.

Tom Paine was a tight-lipped, scurrying little man with a long nose pressed to many grindstones. Born an Englishman and apprenticed early in youth to a corset-maker, he sought relaxation from molding fashionable ladies by attending science lectures in London. It is not unlikely that there he learned the classic bridge designs of Andrea Palladio, the inspiration for the Palladian style of architecture so popular in England. His latent thoughts on the subject bore fruit during a quiet period after he fired the American rebellion. His agile mind and drafting pen produced various plans for intricate wooden bridges. He also designed an iron one in the form of an arch, which he proposed should be built across the Harlem River to the north of New York City. In 1786 he made a model of his bridge and took it to

his patron, Gen. Lewis Morris. However, the General did not advance the money to build it, and the pamphleteer-turned-engineer transferred his energies to Philadelphia.

For weeks he exhibited three versions of his brain child, in model form, to patrons of Peale's Museum. He badgered the city fathers to endorse a scheme for building his bridge across the Schuylkill. True to his patriotic reputation, Paine even suggested a bridge of thirteen arch ribs, one for each of the original states.

But he found Philadelphia money every bit as tight as New York's, and in April, 1787, he disgustedly took his little bridge models and sailed for Europe. In England a bridge of his iron design was actually built, but by the time it was erected the mercurial Paine had bounced off to take part in the French Revolution, and to produce *The Rights of Man* and *The Age of Reason*. Others got both the credit and the lucrative patent rights for his bridge.

Back in Philadelphia, Charles Willson Peale, proprietor of the famous museum, had not forgotten Tom Paine's bridge models. Peale, in addition to enjoying a reputation as a top-flight painter and showman, was another visionary who occupied his spare thoughts on all manner

THOMAS PAINE

of enterprises. In the summer of 1796 he got the idea of building a small footbridge over the street near the State House yard. He produced a quarter-scale model of a novel wooden bridge, using five-foot poplar boards, and placed it in a passage of his museum for all comers to tramp over. Once twelve stout Indians squeezed together to stand on the little model. Peale watched with pride and apprehension, but the bridge did not even quiver.

Pondering the future of the new nation, the middle-aged Peale firmly convinced himself and others that the country urgently needed bridges that would be sturdy as well as cheap to erect, and that would stand secure above floods and frequent ice jams. He abandoned his plans to cross a mere city street and drew details for a single arch to soar across the Schuylkill, and so provide a year-round entry into Philadelphia that would draw trade to and from the West like a magnet.

Charles Peale's drawing shows a gigantic laminated wooden arch, 390 feet in length, made of flat plank wedged and keyed to carry the uphill-and-over roadway. Unusual curved truss panels in the form of a railing braced the arch from above and below. The artist submitted this plan and on January 21, 1797, received the very first United States patent granted for a bridge design. He also incorporated his ideas in a little booklet published the same year and titled *An Essay on Building Wooden Bridges.*

Peale's essay took a dim view of the need to cover wooden bridges, and minimized the rotting action on wood of alternate rains and strong sunlight. He expected to overcome any such deterioration by using tight joints and liberal applications of tar. Hence his plan did not include roof or siding.

Philadelphia was apparently not yet ready to span the Schuylkill, and even Peale's little street bridge was never built. Years later, the the painter's ne'er-do-well son Raphael tried unsuccessfully to erect a bridge on his father's patented design at Beaufort, South Carolina. It failed, insisted Raphael, only "because of too many Yankee workmen."

Although Charles Willson Peale's bridge was never seriously considered as an adequate crossing to lead High Street over the Schuylkill, the mere existence of the model and the promotion of the patent were enough to spur greater interest in replacing the little ferries and inadequate floating bridges which then spanned the river. The Schuylkill Permanent Bridge Company was finally organized March 16, 1798, for the purpose of linking Philadelphia, dryshod, to the West. The magnitude of such an undertaking for that day and age was staggering: its original capital was $150,000. Small wonder that the job took six years!

Philadelphia's Permanent Bridge, as it was always called, came about through the talents of several men used effectively in combination. Each of them deserves much credit for pioneer work in engineering fields scarcely explored up to that time.

*Peale's arch promoted interest in a Schuylkill bridge, but gave way to sturdier plan.*

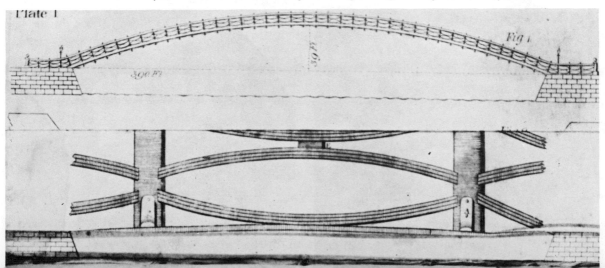

The untiring and resourceful overseer of the new bridge company was its president, Richard Peters, a Philadelphia jurist. Judge Peters' interest in public improvements for his native city was well known, and he took it upon himself to supervise every last detail of construction on the great bridge. It was his ingenuity and tenacity that finally completed the job.

Peters first asked for the services of William Weston, a prominent English engineer who was in Pennsylvania doing canal and turnpike work. Weston presented the company with a draft of a beautiful three-span stone arch bridge, similar to one he had erected over the River Trent at Gainsborough in his native land. It was on this plan that the Schuylkill Permanent Bridge Company expected to build when that first cornerstone was laid with ceremony, and with what John Lewis felt was an adequate inscription, on October 18, 1800.

Work went very slowly. The huge piers in the river presented great problems. For the eastern of the two, foundations were necessary forty-one feet below the surface of the river. But William Weston knew his hydraulics. He devised a plan for a wooden cofferdam of unprecedented size and depth. Boss carpenter Samuel Robinson fashioned the circular dam from some 800,000 board feet of timber, enough to build a good-sized frigate.

Month after month Robinson and Thomas Vickers, the chief stonemason, worked their men from abutment, to piers, and on to the western bank of the Schuylkill. They took

nearly a year to complete each great pile. With progress so painfully snail-paced, the company funds nearly reached a bottom as deep as the river, and Judge Peters had to plead with the stockholders to keep up their subscriptions.

At length plans for an all-stone bridge were reluctantly abandoned. Weston, who had now returned to England, sent detailed drawings for a cast-iron bridge to fit the stone bases, a mode of construction just catching on in the British Isles. The bridge directors regretfully turned this one down as well. There were no foundries in the United States capable of casting iron in such lengths, and importing the segments would have been far too expensive. They decided to erect a wooden structure on the stone piers and abutments.

Once the issue was settled, Peters called in the best long-span wooden bridge man in the country to build the Schuylkill Permanent Bridge. He was Timothy Palmer, a fifty-two-year-old master carpenter and "bridge architect" from Newburyport, Massachusetts, and the first of many New England influences on Pennsylvania bridge building.[*] Palmer, too,

[*] *Covered Bridges of the Northeast*, published in 1957 as the first volume in a projected series on America's great wooden bridges, deals at length with builders and spans of the eight northeastern states. A chapter from it, "The Bones of a Bridge," has been condensed to form Appendix I of this book and describes, with diagrams, the evolution of the bridge truss and the particular contributions made by Timothy Palmer and later builders to this branch of engineering.—R. S. A.

JUDGE RICHARD PETERS

TIMOTHY PALMER

had patented an original bridge design in 1797
—but his spans had not languished on paper.
Rather, his reputation had been made with his
great timber arches over the Merrimack, Ken-
nebec and Connecticut Rivers, fashioned from
naturally-curved trees found in the huge
stands of white pine that covered New Hampshire and the District of Maine. His, too, was
the arched span across the Little Falls of the
Potomac above Georgetown, Maryland. However, Palmer had not built any of these bridges
with roofs.

Palmer, a raw-boned Yankee with hair swept
back over his ears into a queue, brought along
from Newburyport his principal assistant,
Samuel Carr, and four workmen. Together
with local carpenters they proceeded to put up
a three-span, 550-foot arch-truss bridge whose
center span was 194 feet, 10 inches in length.
Unlike Palmer's earlier bridges, in which roadways followed the successive upward curves
of the arches, the flooring of the Permanent
Bridge was only slightly humped. It was 42
feet wide and was divided into two lanes to
avoid the risk of having teams meet at mid-
bridge. The trusswork was far enough along
by January 1, 1805, to open the bridge to traffic. Sawyers and joiners clung to the cross-
beams in the icy Winter air while drays and
carriages passed to and fro below.

At this point, with the great supporting
skeleton all but completed, Timothy Palmer
proudly expected the structure to stand re-

vealed to an admiring populace in general, and
as an advertisement to be examined by building committees on the lookout for a good
bridge designer.

Stubborn Judge Peters had other ideas. He
thought it a shame to leave the bridge's open
framework exposed to the wind and the rains.
He reasoned that weatherboarding the sides
and covering the bridge with a roof would give
long life to this span for which he had labored
so long. He said as much to Palmer; to which
the builder gave an honest answer:

"Relative to the durability of timber bridges
without being covered, sides and top, I answer from experiences I have had.... They
will not last more than 10 or 12 years.... Some
have tried paint in the joints, and others tur-
pentine and oil, but all to no great effect.

"I *am* an advocate for weatherboarding and
roofing, although there are some that say I
argue much against my own interest.... The
Schuylkill Bridge will last 30 and perhaps 40
years if well covered."

His words weren't just idle amiability. Timothy Palmer even agreed to alter his bridge
plans to accommodate such weatherproofing.

That was fine with the Judge. Happily he
sat himself down with a drawing pen to sketch
the cover he envisioned. Now and then he
would stick the pen back in one of the white
tufts over his ear while he sanded the ink and
let it dry. In the end three sketches were proposed for America's first covered bridge. The

*Palmer combined arches and multiple kingposts to support America's first covered bridge.*

*Bridge over the Schuylkill, at Philadelphia.*

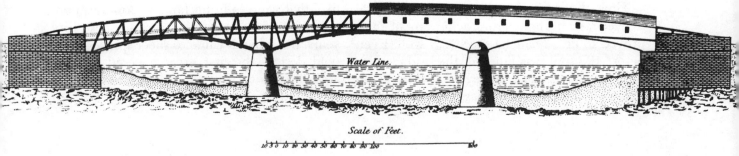

Water Line.

Scale of Feet.

one finally chosen incorporated Judge Peters' ideas, but was drawn by Adam Traquair and a Mr. Dorsey.

Owen Biddle, a prominent Philadelphia architect and builder, was picked to do the actual woodwork to cover the long bridge. He must have felt his responsibility, for the job he did on the Permanent Bridge made it America's fanciest—as well as its first—covered bridge. Along the outside there were simulated colonnades, and forty-four oval windows equipped with shutters. The lower portion of the weatherboarding was fashioned in imitation of masonry, with detailed "stone" blocks to look like arches. As a final touch to heighten the illusion, stone dust was sprinkled on the fresh paint of this section of the bridge.

Nor was this all. By way of celebrating their achievement with the proper embellishment, Judge Peters and the Schuylkill Permanent Bridge Company directors commissioned William Rush, the celebrated naval sculptor, to make two statues in wood to adorn the bridge entrances. Rush, especially famed for his carved and painted figureheads on the USS *Constellation* and many other vessels, obliged with allegorical figures of Agriculture and Commerce at either portal. In addition, on the eastern bank a stone obelisk congratulated the proprietors of the bridge and the builders as "those who by enterprising, arduous and persevering exertions achieved this extremely beneficial improvement." These true sentiments were spelled out in no uncertain terms—and used a lot more letters than John Lewis had thought necessary for his cornerstone six years before.

Thus the great span became an esthetic as well as an engineering achievement, and proved to be a financial success as well. Even before the roof was finished, the bridge company began to make money from tolls. Each teamster and every foot passenger paid hard cash to cross the bridge, and more than $13,600 was collected the first year. The bridge had cost $300,000, all paid by gift or private subscription and with no federal, state or city aid sought or given.

Here was an example of what individual enterprise in America could accomplish. A wonderful and important bridge stretched across the Schuylkill, pointing West, to be used and admired by everyone. Philadelphia was showing the way. Now there would be a grand rush to follow her lead.

Followed it was, by an ever-increasing number of structural masterpieces.

It was the rivers themselves that bred the wooden giants of our Middle Atlantic States. They posed a challenge which the early builders readily accepted, and nowhere else does one find records of so many great arch bridges over such wide and sweeping currents. Most of the longest clear spans—that is, the uninterrupted section of a bridge between abutments not supported by intervening piers—ever erected in wood were built in this area. The longest single-span wooden covered bridge ever built in the world was over Pennsylvania's Susquehanna River at McCall's Ferry, with a clear span of 360 feet, 4 inches. And there were others across the Schuylkill and the Delaware which came close to its record.

This is not to minimize our early builders who laid their roadways doggedly from pier to pier over quietly treacherous waters for lengths reaching up to, and even more than, a mile. Nor does it detract from the covered bridge plans, light, economical and businesslike, that were to bring fame to American engineers and engineering over the next fifty years. But when it came to sheer splendor and bold design, the first great covered wooden arch bridges of this region have never been surpassed.

# II

# Arch, Adze and Genius

WHEN Timothy Palmer finished his great Permanent Bridge the directors of the toll company presented him with a handsome silver tankard and tray, suitably inscribed with their esteem. They also arranged to have a fine miniature of his likeness painted by a visiting French artist. These little extras gave Palmer a high regard for doing business with Pennsylvanians: the only bonus he'd ever received for his labors in New England was a beaver hat.

He had to return for the presentation, because even before he had finished at Philadelphia, he had taken on the job of building a fine two-span arch bridge over the Delaware at Easton, Pennsylvania. He planned to roof this one from the start. The legend ERECTED 1805 T. PALMER on its high enclosed portals looked down on Eastonians for eighty years. This was his second and last covered bridge, for after its completion the inventor-builder spent his last years in semi-retirement at his home in Massachusetts.

More money, plus the challenge of erecting bigger and better bridges, were the inducements that quickly attracted more of New England's self-taught "bridge architects" to Pennsylvania. Among them was Jonathan Walcott, who came down from the rocky hills of Windham in eastern Connecticut when he felt the urge to exercise his talents in greener fields. The bridge design he planned to use was a plain multiple-kingpost truss (see APPENDIX I), supported by bracing from below the bridge floor. His growing reputation, though, was built on three sizable uncovered arch bridges over the lower Connecticut River, with the one at Hartford having the novel arrangment of a tollhouse spang in the middle of the crossing.

Armed with a letter of recommendation from the Governor of Connecticut, Walcott was only thirty-six years old when, in 1812, he made his way to Columbia, Pennsylvania. There a company had been formed to erect and operate a toll bridge over the Susquehanna River. Competition was keen. Three other Connecticut men and two Pennsylvanians also were after the contract. Walcott first cautiously proposed to build only the woodwork of the bridge for the price of $20 a foot. However, after a week of dickering, he found it prudent to team up with the two local mason-carpenters, Henry and Samuel Slaymaker, to bid $150,000 on the entire job and so secure the plum.

*Sheer length—it used 28 piers—gave Walcott's Columbia Bridge its all-time distinction.*

The three certainly earned their money. Although they had no way of knowing it at the time, the Nutmeg-Stater and his colleagues were building the longest covered wooden bridge in the world, for its overall length has never been surpassed in kind. The bridge they erected was well over a mile long—5,690 feet, carried on twenty-eight piers—and was a colossal project for a day when only the power of men and horses was available. In a way the monster bridge was Jonathan Walcott's ultimate effort. Worn out and ill after its completion, he returned to Connecticut and an early death.

Meanwhile Walcott's main competition for engineering superlatives was coming from Theodore Burr, another Connecticut man with a glowing reputation for building bridges.

Theodore Burr deserves a special place of honor among the unsung empire builders of America. He was born at Torringford, Connecticut, in 1771. Despite many rumors to the contrary, Theodore was *not* related to Aaron Burr, but sprang from a family of carpenters and millwrights who took their skills into the wilds of New York State after the Revolution. Burr set up in Oxford, New York, took con-

tracts for bridges all over the state, and his fame grew as fast as the people who used his spans could spread the word. He was a great experimenter, trying all sorts of uncovered trusses, before he finally hit upon a design for a great arch reinforced with kingposts, and supporting a level roadway. This design, patented in 1804, became known as the *Burr truss* (*see* APPENDIX I).

A few busy years later he, too, reached the conclusion that the Commonwealth of Pennsylvania offered the most generous proving ground for his construction theories. The legislature at Harrisburg had authorized four new

*Two views of this unique model made by Burr show his rugged arch-truss.*

private companies to erect bridges over the broad lower Susquehanna at Northumberland, Harrisburg, Columbia and McCall's Ferry—all in Pennsylvania along a hundred-mile stretch of river. Burr managed to snag contracts for building three of the four.

The jobs would require a staggering amount of material, for which the answer was mass production. Burr chose Chenango Point (now Binghamton), New York, for the site of a huge sawmill where he prepared his timbers. From there he hired his own raftsmen to float them down the North Branch and Main River to his bridge sites in Pennsylvania. As for hardware, in his opinion the best iron in the Keystone State came from Centre County; so he made a deal with the ironmasters around Milesburg for all he needed in the way of spikes and bolts.

Burr got to know the bends of the Susquehanna intimately, for he was up and down the river, supervising his masons, raftsmen, carpenters and building crews day after day, month after month—and, as it developed, year after year. The first of these bridges, the one at Northumberland, was begun in 1812, and the last, at Harrisburg, was not completed until 1820.

Any ordinary contractor would have been content to have three big jobs going at once and to cope with all their structural and financial details. But to Theodore Burr, five didn't seem too many. One of the new projects was over the North Branch at Berwick, and the other was in Maryland for still another toll enterprise over the Susquehanna. He also went after the contract for the long crossing at Columbia. Doubtless the directors of the Columbia Bridge Company knew of his many irons in the fire. With all due respect to Burr's ability they figured a sixth bridge would be one too many: they prudently awarded the contract to Walcott and the Slaymakers although his bid was identical in price.

Theodore Burr started at Northumberland, where the village was to be connected with Sunbury to the south by a pair of bridges leap-

frogging over the North Branch. Incidentally, his only competitor for this job had been Robert Mills, an architect and protégé of Thomas Jefferson. Always cheerful in his letters to other bridge companies who were waiting (and had sometimes already paid) for his services, Burr reported early in 1814 that his crew at Northumberland "had got so sprightly that they not only could fling up an arch but also fling one down." It seems that in one of the twin bridges they wedged an arch span so tight that the pressure popped the adjoining one away from the shore abutment. Down the second arch tumbled, sinking the construction gondola below, and then sailed off downstream. The building crew raced after the floating arch and retrieved it. In only two weeks they had it back in place.

Genial Theodore Burr tried to build all five of his Susquehanna bridges at once. The wonder is that he managed to erect even one. He wrote one company: "Gentlemen, your friend T. Burr is perplexed and vexed at least fifty times in one day." Pennsylvania merchants would not accept his scrip from York State banks. Creditors yapped at his heels as he ranged on horseback from the sawmill up in New York down to Tidewater Maryland, paying his men mostly with promises. Burr would get an advance from the Northumberland directors and use it for work on the Harrisburg crossing. When Harrisburg came through with a bit of hard cash, it would be planked down as partial payment to his rough and ready raftsmen.

Although he lost out to Walcott for the distinction of erecting the longest multiple-span covered wooden bridge in the world, the casual genius from Connecticut was to bring off what, in engineering, is regarded as a finer achievement: he designed and built the one with the *longest single span*. This was his bridge at McCall's Ferry, as wild and fearsome a place for crossing a river as even Theodore Burr had ever encountered. For a hundred miles above McCall's the Susquehanna is one

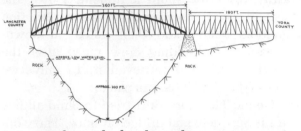

*A tame impression of McCall's Ferry, details of its world's-record arch.*

to two miles wide, but here the great stream is cramped between high hills, so that at low water the run of the river is only 348 feet wide. Burr took depth soundings and whistled with surprise when he came up with a reading of over 100 feet.

The methods he used in building this bridge exemplify the ingenuity and courage with which the old-time masters conquered the difficulties of erecting their giant spans.

His greatest problem was how to place the first huge arch of the bridge from its east shore abutment to a pier built previously in the shallower water toward the west bank.

He knew, of course, that he could never bed temporary supports and scaffolding in a hundred feet of water, so the arch he envisioned would have to be put together from falsework carried on floats. But neither could he string his floats crosswise from abutment to pier in such a current. His solution was to range his floats along the shore for nearly a quarter-mile, spacing them properly with their ends snubbed to projecting rocks on the bank. On each he raised frames that varied in height to correspond with the curve of the arch, whose

huge halves were shaped by broadaxe and adze on the only strip of level land near the bridge site.

The Fall rains came whipping down from the North and the wind howled through the gorge. As the river rose and fell the men kept busy trimming the floats to keep pace with it. One dark night there was a heavy rain and the Susquehanna rose twenty feet. On top of that came a windstorm, sending Burr and his men scurrying from float to float in the gloom, balancing on catwalks over deep water as they braced off and hauled in the ropes that secured the unfinished arch to the comparative safety of the shore. It took them three months to make the arch ready.

Finally, on December 7, 1814, they prepared to swing the arch into place with towlines along the banks. Then a cold snap started ice to forming in the quieter waters to the North. Broken fine on rocks upstream, it jammed some fifteen feet deep in the narrows at McCall's. The floats bucked and twisted and the scaffolding started to split apart. A couple of intrepid workers crossed out onto the hard ice of midstream and rigged a capstan with which to help steady the great arch against being jerked to pieces.

Next came a thaw which lasted until Christmas. Everyone figured that the ice, arch and all, would go at any moment; but about half a mile of it remained at McCall's, with floes from upriver piling into it until the mass loomed ten feet above the shoreline. And right after the Holiday this mountain of ice began to move slowly downstream through the gorge, crushing the floats in its passage. It looked like curtains for the mighty arch, still miraculously undamaged.

Although the jam might only inch its way along—every hour brought the chance of a stiff freeze which would lock it in place once more —it was asking too much merely to stand by while the great curved timbers toppled under the grinding force of the ice pack. Theodore Burr decided on a bold stroke. Why not divide the arch in two and transfer it from the smashed floats onto the ice? Then perhaps it could be slid into place. Eighteen volunteers did the first part of the job, that of bridging an open space offshore. Next they leveled the humped ice mass to make a path and prepared wooden runners to slip under the arch. Time after time the men were up to their armpits in the slushy Susquehanna, and not a word of complaint. Augustus Stoughton was securing ropes up top when his numbed hands lost their grip. Down he went, bouncing twice on the braces, fifty-four feet into a patch of icy open water. He was fished out and got back to work in a few days. His was the only injury recorded on the entire job.

Eight capstans strained as the first half of the arch moved athwart the course of the river. There, firm on the ice, it towered high above the workmen and some fifty riverbank superintendents who had gathered one Sunday afternoon to cheer or jeer, whichever the need turned out to be. They watched as the whole crew was able to slide the arch upstream a total of—four feet.

More manpower would be needed. Burr told the watchers, and they spread the word back into the countryside for miles around. Every farmer needed the bridge, he said, to get his produce and stock to the markets of Philadelphia and Baltimore. He played up sectional rivalry by pitting York County against Lancaster. Local Paul Reveres would ride the back country to rouse Red Lion and Gatchellville, Peach Bottom and Conestoga, telling the farmers to help move the big bridge and "put them Lancaster County (or York) boys to shame!" It was dead of Winter, but forty to a hundred and twenty men showed up every morning and stayed until dark, pushing and hauling with might and main.

Burr made the most of every hand. On the smooth path in the ice he found that, by substituting rollers for runners, it was possible to make moves of up to three hundred feet in a day. At last the abutment and river pier were reached. The crew and their volunteer helpers shoved the other half of the arch into position in only eight days. Moving such an enormous weight—and the structure rose fifty to sixty feet in the air—was no small business. Burr knew he could never have saved and placed his mighty arch without the help of those brawny farmers from both banks of the Susquehanna.

It was braced triangularly in order to become a base from which the rest of the bridge could be built. Then, long after dark of February 1, 1815, the final wedge locked the two halves of the arch together. The last piece of scaffolding fell away, and the arch stood alone. Huge bonfires lit the scene as work-gnarled hands slapped backs and hoisted tankards of rum in a celebration that became a two-day binge. It had taken four months to accomplish what could have been done in four weeks at an ordinary bridge site.

This, however, was no ordinary bridge. It was the longest single-span wooden arch ever built in the world, 360 feet, 4 inches clear span. Today's wooden arches are made from prefabricated laminated timbers. Even these, lifted to position by derrick cranes in the construction of huge blimp hangars and sports arenas, do not equal Burr's McCall's Ferry bridge in length.

Always one for doing things in the grand manner, Theodore Burr claimed that here was one bridge that "God Almighty can not move!"

*"Old Camelback," Harrisburgers' nickname for the western of Burr's tandem bridges, stood until 1903.*

Then he left the finishing to others and was off upriver to see to his other projects. At Harrisburg, solvent for a time, he bought a house on the island midway between his unfinished tandem bridges, certainly an excellent location for impressing visiting building committees. In 1818 the designer-inventor advertised: "I have devoted eighteen years of my life to the theory and practice of bridge building exclusively, during which time I have built forty-five bridges of various magnitudes...."

But creditors were catching up with him, lawsuits were pending and his finances were in terrible shape. The sawmill property in New York State that had cost him $3,400 went for taxes at just $26.50. Burr drove himself in a frenzy. He made new promises, pleading with people who owed him, stalling those he owed, trying in vain to collect royalties on his arch bridge patent.

To add to his troubles, in March of 1818 an unprecedented ice jam came grinding inexorably down the gorge at McCall's Ferry. The stalwart farmers of York and Lancaster gathered, stony-faced, to see the destruction of the bridge on which they had worked so hard. One pious wife watched from high on the bank of the ice-choked Susquehanna as the wonderful arch gave its last splintering crack and commented wryly: "There goes the bridge that God Almighty couldn't move!"

The McCall's Bridge Company never rebuilt, so the stock with which he had been paid was a total loss to Burr. In an effort to recoup, he finished his commitments at Berwick and Harrisburg and snatched at every chance for still more contracts to build smaller bridges.

One of these was for a span over Swatara Creek at Middletown, Pennsylvania. It was here that Theodore Burr suddenly died, only fifty-one years old, late in 1822. Was it an accident or illness? No one knows, and his burial place is unrecorded. There was little money for funeral expenses: the body of this greatest of our pioneer bridge builders probably lies in some Pennsylvania potter's field.

Yet Theodore Burr's arch design became an impressive legacy to new generations of bridge builders. His friends and subcontractors took over where he left off, finished his bridges, and went on to establish firmly the Burr arch-truss as *the* bridge in Pennsylvania, Maryland and the Virginias. In the Midwest the name was often uncapitalized and corrupted to "bur" or "birr." In the Far West any bridge with an arch, no matter what other kind of truss it had, was a "burr," and up in New Brunswick an occasional "Bhurr" truss is still erected. All these hark back to the Yankee who did his finest work in Pennsylvania.

Among his followers was Reuben Field, a Rhode Island man. In 1817 Field took on the erection of the first bridge over the Susquehanna at Derrstown (now Lewisburg), Pennsylvania, when Burr had to admit for once that he was "too busy." Field was also responsible for a long-lived Susquehanna bridge at Wilkes-Barre and for another at Northumberland over the West Branch.

Much-bridged Northumberland—eventually it had seven over the Susquehanna branches and its canals—for a time was the home of

*Reuben Field's Northumberland Bridge.*

James Moore, another enthusiast for the big Burr arch. Born in New Jersey, Moore always considered himself a Pennsylvanian, for his father died when he was a child and young James was bound out to a German cabinet-maker in Northumberland. This apprenticeship was all the education Moore received. His master did teach him to read and write, though —but in German!

James Moore was in his late twenties before he made the changeover from delicate drawer and dowel work to heavy construction with timbers and tenons. Even before Theodore Burr came to Northumberland, Moore had thrown his first bridge over the mouth of Buffalo Creek at Lewisburg. The success of Burr's

design launched James Moore on a far-flung building career. Happily, he was prudent enough to take on only one bridge job at a time. From little crossings close to home, he went on to big ones like the Clarion River Bridge at Clarion, Pennsylvania, built in 1821, and one 1000 feet long and some 40 feet above the waters of Little Conestoga Creek near Lancaster. It was Moore who introduced graceful Burr arches into Virginia bridge building. His was the original Gauley Bridge in that state, over Gauley River on the James River & Kanawha Turnpike. On the same road he also spanned the beautiful Greenbrier River at what is now Caldwell, West Virginia.

In 1832 Jonathan Walcott's over-a-mile-long Susquehanna Bridge was washed away by ice and flood, and Moore went down to Columbia to bid on the rebuilding. Always at a handicap with written English, his proposals were phrased in his own peculiar brand of phonetic spelling. Nevertheless, he was low bidder out of eleven competitors, and for $123,274 Columbia and Wrightsville had the second version of "the longest covered bridge in the world." A slightly different location this time reduced it to a length of 5,620 feet.

Moore, a staunch Baptist, would allow no work to be done on a Sunday. Even pumping stopped, and cofferdams around piers in the

*Moore's replacement for the world's longest covered bridge was burned during the Civil War.*

JAMES MOORE

river were allowed to fill up. At remote bridge sites the contractor would hire an itinerant minister to preach to his workmen each Sabbath day.

After 1845, and until his death ten years later, Moore lived in virtual retirement, devoting most of his time to establishing what is now Bucknell University at Lewisburg. Still, the old gentleman liked to keep his hand in. As late as 1854 he received $48 and a $25 share of stock for plans and specifications on a new bridge to span the Susquehanna at Uniontown (now Allenwood). One of his descendants remarks that he must have used up at least that much in horseshoes and hay during his frequent inspection trips to the site. James Moore's portrait shows a kindly, smooth-faced old man, book in hand, with his spectacles pushed up on his forehead in what was doubtless a characteristic gesture. Bucknell can well be proud of one of its founders, whose success stemmed from filling America's need for sound and adequate bridges.

The last of this region's original master bridge builders was still another outlander, Lewis Wernwag. He was not a Yankee either, but a German immigrant from far-off Reidlingen, Württemberg. Wernwag is believed to have left the valley of the upper Danube and come to this country at seventeen, perhaps to escape the harsh military conscription practiced in the German States at that time.

The new American found a home in Philadelphia, where he was soon showing his mechanical skill in building mills and mill wheels, as well as constructing machinery to make whetstones and nails. The gifted mechanic was forty-one before he designed his first bridge, an ingenious little light timber drawspan to take the Frankford-Bristol Turnpike across Neshaminy Creek northeast of the city of Philadelphia. Recognizing the need for sizable bridges to leap the river barriers of his adopted country, Wernwag decided to study their design and construction. And it was obvious that he would have to build an important bridge to call attention to his talents.

The opportunity was right under his nose. Not content with just Timothy Palmer's Permanent Bridge across the Schuylkill, a group of Philadelphians had organized a company in 1810 to build a second crossing at the site known as Upper Ferry. Architect Robert Mills drew specifications and agreed to act as consulting engineer for the project; but the committee awarded the building contract to Lewis Wernwag on the strength of his successful drawbridge and known mechanical abilities. But the immigrant builder couldn't forego his dream of designing the structure himself, and dazzled Mills with a plan for a bridge with an unprecedented span of over 400 feet. Mills went to bat for Wernwag's idea. The managers would not consent to it, though, and settled on a bold alternate plan—also by Wernwag, and over 300 feet long—as being risky enough.

The cornerstone of the bridge was laid April 8, 1812. Wernwag had considerable trouble making a foundation for the western abutment, and had to use 499 (not 500–499!) piles to reach bedrock. Then began the labor of erecting the second longest single-span covered bridge in the world. It was a huge affair of three arch-trusses, joined without supporting piers and with a roadway that curved up and over. An intricate system of cross-braced wooden panels was connected to the arches by

*Wernwag also built this sturdy highway bridge over the Schuylkill at Philadelphia's City Line near the mouth of Wissahickon Creek.*

cast-iron boxes set into the upper and lower chords (*see* APPENDIX I). The methodical Wernwag sampled all his timbers in advance by sawing through the heart of each huge log in order to detect any unsound wood. Also, after the beams were in place, he insured against dry rot by holding them slightly apart with iron links and screw bolts. An advantage of this procedure was that the bolts could be tightened in case the timbers shrank, and any piece could be replaced without injury to the rest of the bridge.

As the giant span neared completion reports

began to circulate that the bridge of this foreign-born upstart could never stand alone: just take away the scaffolding and watch the whole shebang fall right into the Schuylkill! When the day came for removing the falsework the riverbanks were jammed with people waiting to see the crash. The worried managers had assembled on the porch of nearby Sheridan's Tavern when Wernwag arrived. Their first words were: "Do you think our bridge will stand the test?"

The builder smiled. "Yes, gentlemen, it will."

He then requested them to follow him down to the bridge. Timidly they trooped along behind him onto new-laid planking. At the first set of blocks between arch and falsework, the builder halted. Would one of the managers care to examine the supports?

The man poked at the blocks. "They're all loose!" he exclaimed.

The next set was the same, and the next—all down the line. Since the previous day, the designer told the proprietors, the bridge had been resting on its own abutments. Lewis Wernwag's reputation was made.

The span of the bridge was 340 feet, 3¾ inches from shore to shore. (See frontispiece.) No doubt it reminded local scholars of the immense statue reported to have straddled the harbor of Rhodes in the third century, B.C. It was immediately dubbed The Colossus, and

*Lewis Wernwag patented these three designs, based The Colossus on the center one.*

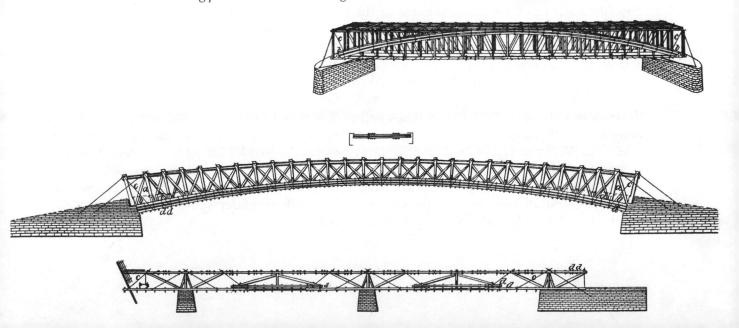

became another Philadelphia brag.

From then on, Wernwag practically had to fight off agents from bridge companies. Usually they would offer a big block of stock in their infant organizations, but sometimes there was cash on the barrelhead. The now famous inventor chose only the best offers, and the next few years found him building bridges across the Delaware at New Hope, over the Schuylkill at Reading and spanning the Susquehanna at Wilkes-Barre. Out in Pittsburgh in 1816 he erected that growing city's first bridges across the Allegheny and the Monongahela.

During this period Wernwag lived at Pawling's Ford, a Schuylkill River town where some Philadelphia capitalists had engaged him to build and manage an ironworks. Here, with what envious industrialists called "extravagant ideas and great expenditure," he put up a dozen shops and dwellings, plus another bridge over the Schuylkill. Wernwag's name for the place was Phoenix Works; today it is the busy workshop boro of Phoenixville. Unfortunately, the state of business after the War of 1812 caused the company to fail. Lewis Wernwag was nearly broke, but ready for a new start: he bought a sawmill on the Susquehanna at Conowingo, Maryland.

In his new location he enlarged the mill to turn out pre-cut timbers which could be rafted down Chesapeake Bay and be made into trestle spans for most of the rivers of Tidewater Virginia and the Eastern Shore. Of course, so that possible customers from the other side of the broad river could come to his mill, Wernwag strung a covered wooden bridge of ten spans across the Susquehanna. He is also credited during this period with building the Market Street Bridge in Wilmington, Delaware, and the curious Belvedere Bridge over Jones Falls in the City of Baltimore.

In 1824 Wernwag transferred his operations to Harpers Ferry, then Virginia. Here he purchased a large island in the Shenandoah River half a mile from its confluence with the Potomac and built a model industrial village which

he called Virginius. Naturally, he bound Harpers Ferry to the Maryland shore of the Potomac River with a new covered bridge. It is believed that he erected another crossing over the mouth of the Shenandoah just below his island settlement.

By now his contracts for bridges were easy to sublet, and needed only the flowing Wernwag signature on a drawing to get it approved by building committees. Dozens of his bridges were actually built by others: by master carpenters like Isaac Nathans, Joseph Thompson, Josiah Kidwell and by his own sons, William and Lewis, Jr. These men, with a cursory visit or two from their mentor, erected the unmistakable "flared kingpost," double- or triple-arch Wernwag bridge from Gunpowder Falls in eastern Maryland to the White River flatlands of central Indiana. They ranged down the Maysville Pike into Kentucky, dotted the National Road across Ohio, and helped carry the Northwestern Turnpike through what is now West Virginia.

Lewis Wernwag also turned his hand to railroad bridges after the iron horse proved its usefulness. His last great work brought the Baltimore & Ohio Railroad clanking across the Potomac into Harpers Ferry. Due to the narrow confines of the riverbanks—which dictated impossibly sharp turns into or out of a normal structure—he made his bridge curve like an S, and added an offshoot at its south end to emit the branch line being built up the Shenandoah toward Winchester. It was a unique piece of covered bridge architecture.

In his years at Harpers Ferry, Wernwag had a hand in building an insignificant structure which, by a quirk of fate, was to become more famous than any of his mighty bridges. It was a little red brick enginehouse for fire-fighting apparatus, and was just one of the United States Arsenal buildings he erected along the Potomac. Sixteen years after his death in 1843, it became forever famous as the improvised fort and surrender spot of Abolitionist John Brown.

III

# Wooden Bridges for Iron Horses

AILROADS use covered bridges? They most certainly did, and in great profusion. Their problem in general was much the same as that of the highways and canals: to take their lines by the shortest possible route from one point to another. A railroad, though, could not accommodate itself to the average highway span; rails had to be continuous and reasonably straight, and they couldn't conveniently be dropped abruptly into a valley and across a bridge set at right angles to a stream. So new bridges had to be built to meet the railroads' special requirements.

It has been said that without its bridges the modern railroad would have been impossible, and without the railroads—such is the intimate connection between them—the modern bridge might never have been known. Thus the railroads and their builders, designing better and stronger bridges through the years, brought the science of bridge engineering in America to successful new heights.

In the Middle Atlantic region the iron horse's job was to connect main cities and to carry men, mail and goods. Philadelphia wished to be linked with Harrisburg, Baltimore with Washington, and Richmond with Danville. Then came the western expansion, with seaboard cities vying to be on the receiving end of trunk routes. It was natural that the first railroad bridges were similar in construction to the highway spans already in existence.

One of railroading's first covered bridges did not carry rails, but conveyed a highway *over* the tracks. This was the well-known Jackson Bridge about two miles out from Baltimore, which took the Washington Pike over the Baltimore & Ohio Railroad. Erected in August of 1829, this overpass was the first railway grade-crossing separation in America.

If Stephen H. Long* had not insisted on a bridge at this point, the B&O would have built the crossing as a tunnel. Long, a ruddy brevet-colonel of United States Army Engineers, was a plodding and honest soldier who had gained considerable renown as an explorer of the Great West. He was forty-five years old when the government pulled him off the Indian trails and assigned him to line up a route for the infant Baltimore & Ohio Railroad Company. Railroad work was all new to the Colonel; still,

* His career and those of Ithiel Town, William Howe and the Stone family are described in greater detail in *Covered Bridges of the Northeast.*

17

he made a habit of self-education both on and off the job, and soon he knew as much of the rudiments of railway alignment and trackwork as did anybody in the United States. Also working for the B&O were two competent civilians, Jonathan Knight and Caspar Wever. They were not quite so economy-minded as the Colonel from New Hampshire was, and for months they argued with Long on the best way to spend the railroad's money. Together the three men planned the route, trooping out, as Long wrote, in "brigades" to size up and map the terrain. But they couldn't agree on what kind of bridges to build.

There was the crossing of Gwynn's Falls, for instance. Knight and Wever, both hailing from Pennsylvania's limestone country, favored a stone viaduct to bridge the 300-foot gap. Colonel Long suggested a sturdy wooden bridge which would save the newly-established company some $71,500. But the starry-eyed B&O directors wanted stone—and they got stone, both for their Carrollton Viaduct at Gwynn's Falls and the long bridge at Relay down the line. These two structures are still standing, but in 1829 it seemed to Stephen Long and a minority of Baltimoreans that those stone bridges cost a fearsome amount of money.

Next came the matter of the stone arched tunnel, projected to avoid crossing the Washington Pike. The Colonel got perturbed all over again, arguing for a vastly cheaper gravel cut and overpass. "Oh, all right!" the directors finally told him. "There's the spot, go ahead and build your blasted covered wooden bridge!"

Long seized the opportunity. By June of 1829 the railroad cut was complete and a detour established. Meanwhile, using mathematical calculations, and without a single precedent for it, the army engineer had designed a panel-truss span to bridge the 110-foot cut. Using green white pine timber, the Colonel and six men framed and raised the little bridge to a position some 40 feet above the railroad bed. It was all done in less than eight weeks, and cost, complete with weatherboarding and a roof, exactly $1,670.

The inventor called America's first overpass the Jackson Bridge in honor of the President. It stood for over thirty years, a vindication of Long's ideas on cheapness and speed in erecting bridges. In 1830 he proceeded to take out a patent on its design. As the *Long truss* it enjoyed popularity with both railroads and highways for well over ten years.

Colonel Long believed his new bridge to be an American necessity. He wrote pamphlets explaining the function of his wooden panel truss—it looked like a series of boxed X's—and issued instructions for erecting it properly. His language contains some rather obsolete terms, but presumably the bridge builders of the 1830's knew all about "joggles" (toothed blocks), "coggles" (iron splices) and "gluts" (screw bolts).

In a carpenter shop on Baltimore's Dark Lane, a strapping Irishman named Thomas Hassard studied the plans used for the Jackson Bridge. In them he saw an opportunity for doubling his business. He knew that Colonel Long was setting up a system of subagents for distribution of the truss patent privileges to prospective builders in all parts of the country. After an interview with the inventor, Hassard came away with the exclusive rights to build Long truss bridges in the State of Maryland.

He found that the B&O was sticking to stone viaducts and trestling. He sold his services instead to another railroad which was struggling to get started—the Baltimore & Susquehanna. In 1832 Hassard put up three 70- to 100-foot railroad bridges for the B&S, all spanning Jones Falls north of Baltimore on the road's original line to Timonium. They are thought to be the first truss bridges built solely for rails.

The Jones Falls jobs were steppingstones to prosperity. Soon the Irish carpenter was "Thomas Hassard & Co., Master Railroad Bridge Builders," with contracts for Long trusses from Virginia to Maine.

Meanwhile the Baltimore & Ohio was inching slowly westward up the Patapsco Valley

*Revamped Harpers Ferry Bridge, looking from Maryland with the Shenandoah River up at the left.*

and over the hills to the promise of trade with the raw western towns. To span the Monocacy River south of Frederick, Maryland, Chief Engineer Benjamin H. Latrobe needed something cheaper than the company's usual stone viaduct and stronger than any of its airy trestlework. He sketched a tentative plan for a wooden truss bridge with the tracks on top, and to build it he called for the services of an old pro: Lewis Wernwag from down in Harpers Ferry. Wernwag's first structure exclusively for railroad use was a 330-foot, three-span arch affair, erected some 40 feet above the Monocacy. It was finished in 1835.

Soon the construction crews were tamping ties and driving rail spikes for miles beyond Monocacy. In apparently no time at all the iron horse would somehow have to be led through the steep defiles of the Potomac and across the river into Harpers Ferry. Here was a serious problem, and again Latrobe had Wernwag work out the details. Railroad, highway and canal must all be cram-jammed onto the narrow ledge at the base of Maryland Heights opposite the Ferry. Wernwag's big double-lane highway structure built eleven years before already occupied the only logical bridge site.

What to do? From pictorial evidence it seems that the old master bridge builder merely adapted his original bridge for railroad use. The old entrance approaches were, of course, far too sharp for trains to negotiate. He overcame the difficulty at the Maryland end by grafting on a new span to angle eastward over the canal. On the Virginia side he attached another section two spans long which would swing the rails westward along the river. Then a new complexity arose when the Winchester & Potomac branch line needed a B&O connection at Harpers Ferry: Since there was no room in the clutter of arsenal buildings on the point of land, Wernwag solved his new problem by building the junction within the bridge, 124 feet out over the Potomac, and adding a spur span to its already giant bulk.

Finished in 1836, the 900-foot Harpers Ferry railroad-highway bridge resembled both an S and a Y. One writer even termed it a "bifurcated bridge." The flanges of B&O locomotives squealed on the rails of the curving east end, and an alert switchman in the gloomy interior set the tracks to debouch trains south to Winchester or west toward Cumberland as they approached the Virginia side.

Philadelphia, meanwhile, had preserved its reputation for unusual crossings over the Schuylkill. This time it was the first covered bridge of more than two spans designed primarily for a railroad.

In 1831, the state-owned Philadelphia & Columbia (now Pennylvania) Railroad was seeking an entrance into the city from the

*Cables ease loaded cars down the inclined plane toward John Babb's huge Belmont Bridge.*

northwest. To create it they built an inclined plane down to the Schuylkill at Belmont, and contracted with John Babb of Wilkes-Barre for a bridge angled across the river at Peters Island to carry their rails on into the city. Babb built for the company an immense double-barreled, seven-span structure 1,018 feet long. The south lane was laid with tracks and the other served as a common roadway. Sandwiched between the two, and flanked by the great supporting beams, was a long dark footwalk for pedestrians. Babb used Burr arches in giving the City of Brotherly Love its third example of pioneer wooden trusswork.

The great structure was painted a somber red, and soon became known as the Columbia Bridge because of its railroad connection with the West (not to be confused with the mile-long bridge over the Susquehanna at Columbia). Eventually it was acquired by the Reading Railroad. It stood for over half a century. At the time it was replaced by an iron crossing in 1886, John Babb's masterpiece was Philadelphia's oldest and last surviving covered bridge over the Schuylkill.

Wooden arches sprang up elsewhere in Pennsylvania during the 1830's to serve the infant rail lines, and their timbers creaked under the weight of increased tonnage from Easton to the Ohio line. Henry R. Campbell built some fine Burr-type bridges for the Reading's right-of-way. Others carried the Pennsylvania's main line over important streams like Sherman's Creek and the Juniata River. Across the North Branch of the Susquehanna two multiple-arch bridges with fancy portals gave Philadelphia & Erie passengers a dark and smoky entry into Northumberland. These were some of the good ones.

But in the northern part of the state the Erie Railroad erected covered wooden arch bridges with unhappy results. A standard bridge for the Erie was developed in 1847 by the road's chief engineer, Maj. Thompson S. Brown. Consulting with him was Horatio Allen, whose early locomotive experiments and railway design have given him deserved and lasting fame. When it came to planning bridges, however, Brown and Allen were less than adequate. They dreamed up a multiple-kingpost bridge with heavy chords and light counterbracing. For strength they added great arches of laminated plank. Knotless white pine and oak timber were employed, and the roof and clapboards were given three coats of good white lead. All this was fine, and the bridges must have been handsome to look at—at first.

To understand the weakness of their design, we can take time out and consider what a bridge truss really does. In APPENDIX I you will

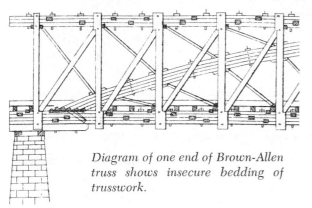

*Diagram of one end of Brown-Allen truss shows insecure bedding of trusswork.*

find an explanation of the principles used in building our early bridges. For now, though, we can say simply that a good truss, whose ends are properly bedded in its abutments, does not prop, it *shoves*. As a load passes over the bridge, the apparently rigid truss members come alive and the great timbers squeeze and pull against each other; the whole superstructure presses harder into the banks, and so its strength actually increases.

Where Brown and Allen made their big mistake was in failing to bed the ends of the arches properly. Instead of attaching the butts of their bowed timbers deep in the masonry below the bridge, these otherwise capable engineers tied the arches to the lower stringers with iron straps, and rested the ends either on *top* of the abutments, or, worse yet, several feet out from them. Their flimsy method, seen in the sketch above, should be contrasted with solid trusswork bedding (e.g. as shown on page 27).

The Erie put up Brown-Allen arch-trusses over every sizable creek on its Pennsylvania right-of-way from Sawmill Rift to Great Bend. Included were big ones over the Delaware, the D&H Canal, and the Susquehanna. The first travelers on this route noted that the bridges "shook notably," and later, "alarmingly." In a year or so the bridges were real shook: the pounding from trains inched the trusses off the abutments, the chords cracked at the arch bases, and, with devious strains, the timbers began to snap at unexpected spots. Erie maintenance men had one prolonged headache as

minor wrecks began to occur at its bridges; one span even fell of its own weight without a locomotive in sight. The company was in financial straits and the management was at odds with the engineers. Desperately, the men in charge put shoring and bents under the faulty spans, and replaced several with a new and untried patent iron bridge. The wooden ones that still remained presented a decrepit appearance for years, propped like limping dowagers trying to keep their skirts out of the water. The Erie's standardization proved to be premature.

The hunt continued for an ideal railroad bridge, what with companies expanding all over the Eastern Seaboard. Many types of bridge structure were employed with varying success. One interesting example was the 300-foot, two-span wooden contraption built across the Patapsco River at Elysville (now Alberton), Maryland.

This bridge was the invention of Benjamin H. Latrobe, whom we have already encountered working with Lewis Wernwag on the Monocacy and Harpers Ferry bridges. Latrobe was the son of an illustrious architect, and was no mean hand with ruler and calipers himself. He held down his job as the B&O's chief engineer for some twenty-two years, dominating the line's engineering and pushing its rails through to the Ohio River in the face of tremendous difficulties. Latrobe's bridge work seems to have been confined to design, and others transformed his plans into wood. Well-known truss inventors like Wendell Bollman and Albert Fink got their basic training in bridge building at the B&O shops under Latrobe.

For the bridge that brought him the most credit, Ben Latrobe copied, modified and adapted printed plans of the famous covered wooden bridge which once stood over the Rhine at Schaffhausen, Switzerland. More or less an enlarged queenpost truss, it was an intricate thing, with numerous keys, wedges and blocks to hold it together. James Murray, chief assistant on the job, erected the first one over

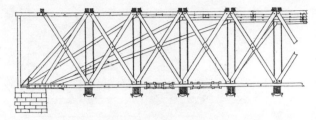

*Cutaway model of Latrobe's Elysville Bridge and part of its unsuccessful "little Schaffhausen" design.*

the Patapsco in 1838–39. It had a unique innovation: an inside ceiling of sheet iron to protect the vulnerable roof from the sparks of chuffing wood-burners. Ben Latrobe had heard that the trotting of a dog over the Swiss Schaffhausen bridge had caused it to tremble. He was quite pleased when his American replica supported a test load of seventy tons of train.

A similar bridge of Latrobe's had a less auspicious inauguration. In 1851, with the assistance of Albert Fink, he put up a four-span wooden bridge over the North Branch of the Potomac beyond Cumberland. The engineer invited a number of young students from various technical schools to witness the first test of the long structure. The bridge had not yet been weatherboarded, so the boys could cling to the sides with the tracks at eye level. Spouting sparks and steam, a 25-ton B&O Camel engine trundled slowly across. To the students' surprise the floor sagged and rose visibly, both ahead and behind the locomotive. Ben Latrobe laughed at their consternation, and assured them there wasn't the least bit of danger. But one of the tyro engineers wrote in his journal:

*Benjamin H. Latrobe, Jr.*

"I failed to be convinced that this was a good bridge!"

It decidedly wasn't. For six years it swayed and undulated under the passage of B&O freights and varnish. Albert Fink was a bit ashamed to have his name painted as "Asst. Engineer" over the portals. While Latrobe was busy elsewhere on consulting work he quietly took the offending structure down and replaced it with a sturdy iron bridge which was fully his own design and responsibility.

Nine out of thirteen of the Latrobe-inspired bridges on the B&O had to be replaced in twelve years. Even the Elysville (little Schaffhausen) bridge over the Patapsco—a handsome structure, but difficult to keep in trim—literally shook itself apart by 1853. Ben Latrobe specialized in tunnel work after that. He was a fine engineer, who deserves to be remembered for other things than his bridges.

More successful was Ithiel Town, a gifted architect from New Haven, Connecticut. In 1820 he had devised and patented a new and unheard-of type of bridge. It used no arches, no exterior supports: it was simply a latticework of thick wooden planks, pinned together with round pegs called "trunnels" (*see* APPENDIX I). Despite its flimsy appearance the Town lattice made a good bridge, and dozens upon dozens of New England builders willingly paid the inventor $1 a foot for the privilege of erecting them. Town grew rich on his bridge royalties, and with the advent of railroads saw further opportunity to promote his patent "mode." He condensed his lattices tighter together, like the crisscross network of a fancy piecrust, and figured, rightly, that so doubling his truss would make his bridge strong enough to sup-

MONCURE ROBINSON

into railway and bridge company directors' meetings, and at the slightest provocation he'd make a pitch for his patent bridge. In Philadelphia he found a master carpenter, Amos Campbell, who could execute his designs to perfection. Campbell put up bridges on Town's "mode" over the Schuylkill at the Falls, over the Delaware at Centre Bridge and Yardleyville, and over the Conestoga at Lancaster.

Town and Campbell tried hard in 1832 to win the contract for replacing Walcott's mile-long bridge across the Susquehanna at Columbia, Pennsylvania. The inventor gave an impassioned plea for acceptance of his bid, and offered to waive the sizable royalty which would be due him for building so huge a structure. Mr. Town's entreaties fell on deaf ears. The Columbia proprietors were satisfied with the familiar arch and distrusted any "garden-fence type of bridge out of New England."

port the passage of trains.

Then he set out for Pennsylvania, where some big railroad bridges obviously were going to be needed. The early 1830's saw Ithiel peddling his wares in the whole stretch of country between the Delaware and the James. A cocky little redhead, Town would stick his long nose

However, the Connecticut architect did find a staunch ally in Moncure Robinson, a young Virginian who had studied engineering in Europe. Returning to this country, he was in great demand for his knowledge of French and British railway practice. He was only

*Robinson's husky lattice carried R&P rails more than half a mile across the James River to Richmond.*

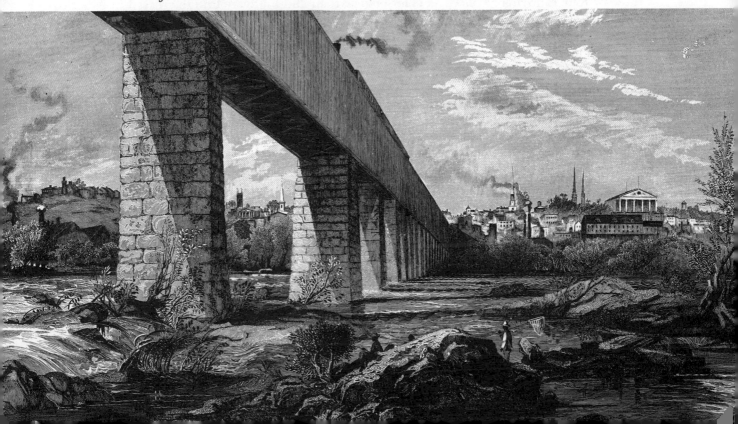

*Gray's Ferry and, right, its obelisk.*

thirty-two years old when, in 1834, he was put in charge of building the Philadelphia & Reading Railroad. At first he tried stone bridges, but was quick to see that they would be far too costly for their time and place. Then he adopted Ithiel Town's lattice construction. For some years this type predominated on the Reading, and Robinson was always quick to defend it. In railroad bridges of more than one span, he declared, the feature of Town's continuous lattice construction added greatly to the strength of the whole.

Robinson also acted as consultant for other lines and was sometimes in charge of building three or four railroads at once. As chief engineer of the Richmond & Petersburg Railroad he introduced the Town plan into Virginia with an immense nineteen-span, 2,844-foot railroad bridge some 60 feet above the James River at Richmond. The dynamic little Virginian was also influential in making the Town

bridge a standard design on the early railroads in the Old Dominion, particularly the Richmond & Danville, and the Virginia Central.

Two more notable lattice bridges on Keystone State railroads resulted from Ithiel Town's oratory and finger-shaking in the board rooms.

One created a new southern approach to Philadelphia at Grays Ferry to bring the Philadelphia, Wilmington & Baltimore line into the city. This was a double-barreled, five-span, 800-foot combination railroad and highway bridge, built in 1837–38. The railroad company directors were mighty proud of it and formally dubbed the bridge The Newkirk Viaduct in honor of their president, Matthew Newkirk. In the best Philadelphia tradition they even erected a stone obelisk on the south bank to commemorate the "grand achievement." But people never took to the new name: the structure was known as Grays Ferry Bridge and is still so called today.

The other big Town bridge was strung across the Susquehanna River by the Cumberland Valley Railroad, to put its line into Harrisburg. Built by William Milnor Roberts of Philadelphia in 1835–36, it was the first combined railroad and highway bridge erected in America. A single railroad track ran on the nearly flat roof, and there were two lanes of roadway inside. The original spans burned in 1844 and were immediately replaced by another 4,277-foot lattice structure on the twenty-two piers, just below Theodore Burr's old island-strad-

*Part of Burr's tandem crossing rises behind this view of America's first rail-highway combination.*

*Inflexible Arched Truss used to carry Erie RR rails over the Delaware to York State; below, McCallum during the War as head of U.S. Military Railroads.*

dler. One of the foremen on this new job, Samuel Hege of Chambersburg, Pennsylvania, was all of nineteen. He was later to carry the Town lattice truss far beyond Pennsylvania—westward through Ohio and into Indiana.

The story is told of an elderly York County farmer who, in those early days of railroads, had never seen that novelty—a train. He started off for Harrisburg one morning with the avowed intention of examining an iron horse. On the Bridgeport side of the Susquehanna River he entered what appeared to be an ordinary covered bridge with a rather flat roof. Suddenly there was a terrible rumbling overhead, accompanied by a scream and a hoot. Convinced he was bewitched, the man hauled his wild-eyed horse about in the narrow lane and lit out down the pike. Not until a mile out of town did the farmer realize what had panicked him: proceeding in its splendor along rails laid on top of the bridge had been the very locomotive he had come to see.

Up North the Erie Railroad was still having bad luck with both its wooden and iron bridges. The Brown-Allen trusses shook to pieces, and many of the iron replacements were built too tight to their abutments, buckling and snapping as they expanded with Summer's heat. Down the line a burly young Scotsman, Daniel McCallum, thought he could remedy the Erie's bridge woes. He was a bridge carpenter employed by the railroad, with plenty of chances to experiment with models. He tested all types of trusses and came up with one of his own, which he patented in 1851 as McCallum's Inflexible Arched Truss. His bridge design called for a deeper truss than most, one made possible by a curved upper chord. On each side extra bracing fanned down from the bow of the chord and slanted into a funnel-like iron holder which in turn was cemented into the masonry of the abutments.

After an impressive test at Lanesboro, Pennsylvania, where an "inflexible" safely carried four heavy engines, the McCallum invention became the Erie's most-used bridge. Within seven years there were over a hundred on the line, and their popularity spread from Quebec to Missouri, and even to faraway Australia. McCallum gained quite a reputation for his patent truss. He became superintendent of the Erie, president of his own bridge building firm, and a major-general in the Union Army's railroad construction corps during the Civil War.

The "inflexible" truss was indeed an exceedingly stiff and adequate railway structure when it was built under McCallum's direction. But the complications of putting one together stumped ordinary carpenters. One engineer even went so far as to hire a ballroom and make full-sized drawings on the smooth floor in order to work out patterns for framing a McCallum bridge. The use of the invention languished, and on his return from the War General McCallum saw the handwriting on the wall. He could no longer compete with the builders of iron bridges.

Paradoxically, one particular new and sound design in wood was the pilot model for trusses in metal.

In mid-century the Burr arch, Long's panel and the Town lattice—all of them as used for railroad structures in Pennsylvania, Maryland and the Virginias—were rudely swept aside by a whirlwind invasion from the North. What the railroads had needed all along and not found was an uncomplicated wooden bridge that could be erected and maintained easily. William Howe, a Massachusetts carpenter-builder, supplied the answer in 1840. He patented a panel job of wooden chords and braces, but held top to bottom by vertical iron tension rods. Built in a hurry or with unseasoned timber, Howe truss bridges could be adjusted with ease by merely turning nuts, and tightening turnbuckles. The far-reaching importance of his invention is little realized today, but it is safe to state that without Howe's bridge thousands of miles of American railroads just wouldn't have ever been built.

Like Ithiel Town, William Howe was a promoter who sold the rights to build bridges on his patented design. He divided the country into territories and apportioned exclusive franchises among his numerous relatives and close friends in the New England bridge building fraternity. Howe's brother-in-law, Daniel Stone of Springfield, Massachusetts, got the rich prize of the State of Pennsylvania. In 1848 he began a mammoth bridge north of Harris-

burg over that well-known challenge to builders, the Susquehanna River. To carry the Pennsylvania Railroad across at Rockville, he used twenty-three spans for an overall length of 3,670 feet. It was a deck bridge—i. e., the Howe trusses were *under* the roadway in all but a portion across the canal—and each span was stiffened by the addition of arches. A violent tornado in March of 1849 whirled away and shattered six unfinished spans. Stone nevertheless completed the bridge on schedule, and it stood steadfast against Susquehanna freshets for twenty-eight years.

Neighboring rail lines quickly saw the advantages of the Howe construction, and Dan Stone added Maryland and Virginia to his territory. He was besieged with new business. The Reading, the Wilmington & Baltimore, and a score of little Virginia lines began using Howe trusses instead of Town's "mode." Even the Baltimore & Ohio, not yet quite sure of iron, wanted some. With all the work of parceling out contracts and collecting royalties, Stone could hardly find time to take a contract himself.

When he did, it was for another big one, right in the heart of Philadelphia. The Philadelphia & Columbia Railroad had long been wanting a new entrance to the city that would

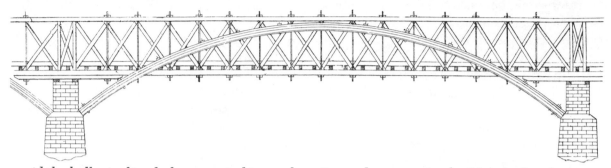

Daniel Stone's P&C bridge at Market Street, above, added arches to Howe's panels and tie-rods, below.

avoid the balky inclined plane created to reach Babb's old rail span at Belmont. Finally the company obtained the rights to Timothy Palmer's old Permanent Bridge at Market Street. Dan'l Stone proposed a new, level-floored structure on the Howe truss plan to replace America's first covered bridge, and secured the contract to build it in 1850. His Market Street Bridge of that year was a huge thing, wide and commodious enough for railroad, vehicular and pedestrian traffic. The long, high bridge had a wide roof but little siding, so travelers were afforded a good view of the river front as the trains snorted into the city, and prospective builders had a chance to examine Howe's interesting new truss design.

Daniel Stone was a busy man for over ten years, stumping the countryside from the Delaware to the Ohio River country in search of business, letting subcontracts and collecting his royalties. With the start of the Civil War he plunged into work for the Union armies, rebuilding bridges destroyed in the wake of battle. For some still unexplained reason he ended his own life in 1863, at the height of his career.

Other communities in Pennsylvania had unusual covered railroad bridges. One of the

No sleep at the switch: Easton-Phillipsburg spans shuffled three railroads on two levels.

oddest stretched interstate between Easton and Phillipsburg, New Jersey. A connection between the Jersey Central, Lehigh Valley and Belvidere Delaware Railroads, it carried tracks both on top and between the trusses. In effect, its spans formed not merely a Y, but made a complete triangle on two levels. On the east end the lower line diverged at an angle from the main structure by using a section two spans long to reach the Jersey shore; meanwhile another bridge section immediately to the north (in New Jersey) crossed the Morris Canal and ducked under the upper level tracks. Yardmen switching trains on and off this Easton Bridge must have gone quietly mad!

At Glen Onoko, Pennsylvania, the Jersey Central's route crossed the Lehigh River and pierced Moyer's Rock, a mountain wedged tight against the churning stream on the opposite shore a little above Mauch Chunk. The Central blasted a tunnel through the rock to connect with a two-track river crossing. The result was a covered bridge leading directly into a mountain. Summer vacationers at Glen Onoko recall the puffing little Central trains whose cars were loaded with laughing chil-dren on a day's excursion. Sight and sound of the gaily chattering crowd would be cut off completely as the engine gave a parting whistle and entered the bridge.

"I always felt," a mother once said as she recalled those days in the '70's, "as if the Pied Piper had taken my children and disappeared inside the mountain!"

Over the years the covered railroad bridges in the Middle Atlantic States have vanished, although not so abruptly as the trains did on leaving Glen Onoko. On the lines carrying lumber in the Alleghenies they gave staunch service down into the present century. The Reading had a few on branches until the 1930's. A notable one was the skewed bridge covered with sheet iron, at Huntingdon Valley not far from Philadelphia. It was a Reading bridge that was the last in the region to go— the old Burr arch bridge over Swatara Creek near Pine Grove, Pennsylvania. For well over twenty years now, people from this area who want to see a covered railroad bridge have had to travel far afield to Vermont and New Hampshire, or even to Washington and Or-egon, to find one.

*Moyer's Rock emits a Jersey Central train headed for Glen Onoko station while, in the background, Lehigh Valley RR passengers arrive less dramatically. From a nineteenth-century vacation brochure.*

# IV

# Battles and Burning Bridges

MILITARY ACTIONS which involved covered bridges were commonplace during the Civil War. Once-friendly spans, their cool shadows turned sinister, were fought over, destroyed and rebuilt by both great armies during the four years of the world's first modern war. All over the South they carried main highways, particularly along the invasion routes through Virginia: they crossed the Potomac at Washington, Berlin and Harpers Ferry, and the James at Richmond and Lynchburg. In the western counties they led turnpikes over the West Fork, the Gauley, the Shenandoah and the Cheat. But skirmishes were not confined to highway bridges. Rail-

roads were vital to the movement of men and matériel, and accordingly their covered bridges assumed strategic importance in determining the locations of many battles.

It was a covered railroad bridge, an important one, that figured in one resounding incident preceding the War. On October 16 and 17, 1859, John Brown raided Harpers Ferry, Virginia, and seized the government arsenal and rifleworks.

His men also took possession of Lewis Wernwag's big S-shaped bridge over the Potomac. A look at the rough sketch below shows why they did.

The point of land where the main action at

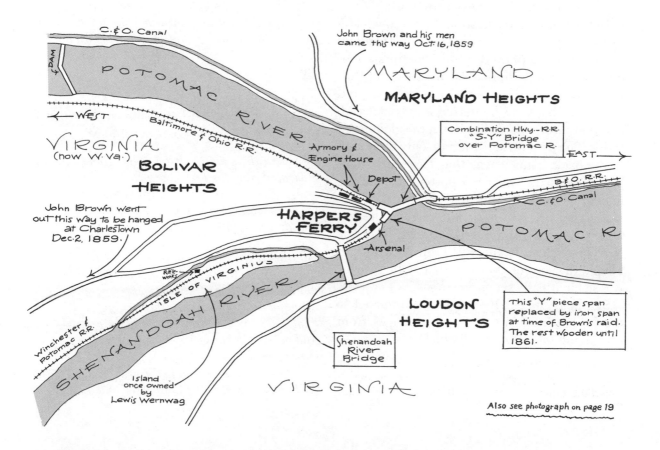

*Also see photograph on page 19*

Harpers Ferry took place was a welter of rivers, bridges and railroad tracks. The arsenal, enginehouse and armory were strung along the Virginia shore of the Potomac between the river and the center of town. The rifleworks, however, was situated on the island in the Shenandoah River where Wernwag had begun his industrial village and made his home. His long covered highway bridge from the foot of the island over to frowning Loudon Heights was destined to play only a minor part in the raid. Not so the old Potomac span: it offered the best means of retreat back to the Maryland hills. And controlling the bridge gave Brown's men another advantage. We have seen how Wernwag revamped it, adding spurs to swing rails onto it from three directions; now, twenty-three years later, its strange construction was to provide the setting for a tragic ambush.

The raiders huddled within its bulk as the Wheeling-Baltimore express pulled in from the west for a midnight stop at the station near the bridge's mouth. Keyed to an almost unbearable pitch by their leader, they started firing.

In the rain and dark, shots began to whistle by the panting locomotive. The train's conductor prudently kept his distance, but the stationmaster's servant slipped off his shoes and offered to see what the trouble was. As he neared the bridge he was silhouetted in its open end, and there were more shots from the gloomy interior. The man turned and ran, only to be shot in the back. Thus it was that Heyward Shepherd, freedman and B&O porter, became the first to die. Later, the first of Brown's men, Dangerfield Newby, was killed when the Jefferson Guards captured the bridge from the Maryland side. Ironically, both Newby and Shepherd were of the race that "Old Brown" was so fanatically set on freeing.

Stephen Vincent Benét gives full impact to the bridge incidents, in these passages from his stirring *John Brown's Body:**

*From *John Brown's Body*, Rinehart and Co., Inc., copyright 1927, 1928 by Stephen Vincent Benét; copyright renewed 1955, 1956 by Rosemary Carr Benét.

*A little later*
*It was Patrick Higgins' turn. He was the night-watchman*
*Of the Maryland Bridge, a tough little Irishman*
*With a canny, humorous face, and a twist in his speech.*
*He came humming his way to his job.*
*                    "Halt!" ordered a voice.*
*He stopped a minute, perplexed. As he told men later,*
*"Now I didn't know what 'Halt!' mint, any more*
*Than a hog knows a holiday."*
*                    There was a scuffle.*
*He got away with a bullet-crease in his scalp*
*And warned the incoming train. It was half-past one.*
*A moment later, a man named Shepherd Heyward,*
*Free negro, baggage-master of the small station,*
*Well-known in the town, hardworking, thrifty and fated,*
*Came looking for Higgins.*
*                    "Halt!" called the voice again,*
*But he kept on, not hearing or understanding,*
*Whichever it may have been.*
*                    A rifle cracked.*
*He fell by the station-platform, gripping his belly,*
*And lay for twelve hours of torment, asking for water*
*Until he was able to die.*

Then, after describing how Kagi—"who, with two others, held the rifle-works"—urged Brown to retreat, the poem continues:

*Of course they were cut off. The whole attempt*
*Was fated from the first.*
*                    Just about noon*
*The Jefferson Guards took the Potomac Bridge*
*And drove away the men Brown posted there.*

*There were three doors of possible escape*
*Open to Brown. With this the first slammed shut.*
*The second followed it a little later*
*With the recapture of the other bridge*
*That cut Brown off from Kagi and the arsenal*
*And penned the larger body of the raiders*
*In the armory.*
*                    Again the firing rolled,*
*And now the first of the raiders fell and died,*

*Dangerfield Newby, the freed Scotch-mulatto*
*Whose wife and seven children, slaves in Virginia,*
*Waited for him to bring them incredible freedom.*

Thus a famous poet describes the raid's first two casualties.

Other historians hold that Higgins, the watchman, was held captive until after the train stopped; that Heyward Shepherd (as his name is given on the marker erected at Harpers Ferry by the United Daughters of the Confederacy) was not challenged but was shot by a trigger-happy raider as his form was outlined in the mouth of the bridge, and that the loss of the "other bridge"—the one over the Shenandoah—couldn't have cut Brown off from the arsenal.

Men's memory of the facts, names and anatomy connected with great events becomes clouded with continuous retelling. Also, the geography of the town was such that it is difficult to say exactly where Brown and his lieutenants were stationed at any given time during the action. This book is not concerned with weighing one detail of the tragedy against another: it offers these accounts only to show how History made use of Lewis Wernwag's big somber crossing over the Potomac River.

Farther west, in an area that was part of Virginia as the Civil War began—West Virginia did not become a separate state until 1863—was a small town called Philippi. Although much of the western portion of the state was pro-Union, a Confederate encampment of local cavalry and militia was established in Philippi under the command of able Col. George A. Porterfield. Porterfield had orders to seize the whole western section of the Baltimore & Ohio Railroad's lines, from Grafton to Parkersburg and up to Wheeling: a tall order for a commander with less than eight hundred men, very few guns, and a great deal of unusable ammunition. Nevertheless Porterfield did manage to perform an Act of War. On May 27, 1861, he dispatched Col. William J. Willey and two men on a train toward Wheeling, and the three deliberately burned two

wood-and-iron railroad bridges near Mannington, Virginia. Another group set fire to three scattered bridges on the Parkersburg line. The next day Southern partisans, bent on cutting communications to the East, burned Patterson's Creek Bridge on the B&O, as well as the canal span of the Potomac crossing south of Cumberland, Maryland.

When Gen. George B. McClellan, over in Cincinnati, heard about the burnings he began moving Ohio and Indiana troops into the area to put a stop to such doings. Colonel Porterfield got word that the Federals were on their way to trap him at his headquarters; but he delayed his retreat too long.

On the night of June 2nd his patrols were posted carefully on the one road that the Union forces were *not* using to approach Philippi and the Confederates retired to their billets—a few tents, the courthouse, private homes and barns. They even spread their blankets in the dry confines of the big two-lane covered bridge that was built in 1852 to span Tygart's Valley River at the village entrance. Half-hearted guards closed off one lane of the bridge for the comfort of their sleeping comrades, and patrolled the other dark entrance in the mud and pouring rain. Miserable enough, they were unaware that at four o'clock in the morning thirty-seven companies of Union troops, led by seven eager colonels, were making a rendezvous to surround the town and capture them.

Two Federal cannon were mounted on a hill in readiness to bombard Philippi as soon as a

pistol shot signaled that all the forces had arrived. The attack was still in the offing when a Confederate sympathizer, Mrs. Thomas Humphreys, took a potshot at some passing soldiers; and the cannoneers let go. Down in Philippi the sleeping Southerners roused and ran. Those who had horses spurred them southward, followed by foot soldiers running pell-mell down the Beverly Pike. The guards abandoned the covered bridge, and Col. Ebenezer Dumont's Seventh Indiana Volunteers "captured" it, intact. The battle produced only three casualties, and is sometimes called "The Philippi Races," but General McClellan wrote such glowing reports of the skirmish that it was hailed throughout the North as a major victory.

Philippi's covered bridge still stands today on busy U.S. 250. Nearly a century after the event, it carries this legend inscribed on its portals: SCENE OF THE FIRST LAND BATTLE OF THE CIVIL WAR.

Six hundred fresh Indiana troops took part in a skirmish the next week. They were volunteer Zouaves stationed at Cumberland, Maryland, under command of Col. Lew Wallace (later to become famous as author of *Ben Hur*). They set out by rail for Romney, Virginia, left their train, and marched all night in order to surprise the town at eight o'clock in the morning. Met only by scattered fire, the Zouaves waved their hats and dashed across the covered bridge over the Potomac into Romney in time to eat the breakfast prepared for the fleeing Johnny Rebs.

War was just a grand lark in those first few months of the conflict, and armies had not fully learned the importance of burning their bridges behind them.

Little railroad bridges destroyed by Southerners up the branch lines in Virginia were quickly being replaced with trestling. So, on June 14, 1861, the Rebels took a drastic step: this time they cut the main line of the Baltimore & Ohio Railroad only sixty miles from Washington. To do it, they blew up and burned the big Harpers Ferry Bridge where John Brown had struck his blow two years before. Earlier, at the Opequan crossing, the Confederates burned a long covered B&O bridge and dropped it fifty-six feet into a deep gorge, and on top of the blazing timbers they tumbled fifty loaded coal cars; the smoldering heap burned for two months.

The Baltimore & Ohio was, because of the logistics of this new kind of warfare, in the

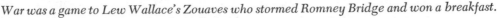

*War was a game to Lew Wallace's Zouaves who stormed Romney Bridge and won a breakfast.*

*A main span of Harpers Ferry Bridge blows sky-high for the benefit of* Harper's Weekly *readers.*

THE UNION     versus     SECESSION.

The Union Builds Bridges.     and     Secession Destroys Them.

*Haupt torpedoes, open and assembled.*

A simple and expeditious mode of destroying bridges and rendering locomotive engines useless to an enemy, is often a desideratum. Cavalry may penetrate far into an enemy's country, may reach bridges forming viaducts on important lines of communication, which it may be desirable to break effectually, or, in retreat, the destruction of a bridge may be essential to the safety of an army, and yet time may not be sufficient to gather combustibles, or they may not be accessible, or the fire may be extinguished, or the damage may be so slight as to be easily repaired.

What is required is a means of certainly and effectually throwing down a bridge in a period of time not exceeding five minutes, and with apparatus so simple and portable that it can be carried in the pocket or a saddle-bag.

These requirements are fulfilled by a torpedo which consists simply of a short bolt of seven-eighths inch iron, eight inches long, with head and nut—the head to be two inches in diameter, and about one inch thick. A washer of the same size as the head must be placed under the nut at the other end, with a fuse-hole in it. Between the washer and the head is a tin cylinder one and three-quarters inches in diameter, open at both ends, which is filled with powder, and, when the washer and nut are put on, forms a case which encloses it.

In using this torpedo, a hole is bored in a timber; the torpedo (head downwards) is driven in by a stone or billet of wood, and the fuse ignited. The explosion blows the timber in pieces, and, if a main support, brings down the whole structure.

The time required is only that which is necessary to bore a hole with an auger. Ordinary cigar lighters, which burn without flame, and cannot be blown out, are best for igniting the fuse, which should be about two feet long.

For portability, the auger should be short, say thirteen inches, and the handle movable and of the same length.

The proper place at which to insert the torpedo is of much consequence. Most of the Virginia bridges are Howe trusses without arches. In this kind of bridge, the destruction of the main braces at one end, and on only one side of a span, will be sufficient to bring down the whole structure. There are usually but two main braces in each panel, and two torpedoes will suffice to throw

thick of the blows dealt by opposing armies. With the end of 1861 all but one of its bridges between Cumberland and Berlin had been destroyed. Indignant Northern newspapers ran cartoons to the effect that "Union builds bridges," while "Secession destroys them."

It wasn't long before righteous Yankees lost their scruples and took a leaf from the "Sesesh" book. November 1, 1862, is the date on the War Department's instructions for a mean and fast way to destroy wooden bridges. The little manual is signed "H. Haupt, In charge of U.S. Military Railroads," who describes his methods with chilling matter-of-factness:

down a span. Two men can bore the two holes at the same time without interfering with each other.

Cartridges containing a fulminate would be more portable, but they are not always conveniently procurable, and their use is attended with risk of explosion.

It is only necessary to operate at one side and on one end of a bridge. If one side falls, the other side is pulled down with it.

If the structure contains an arch, two additional torpedoes will be required; but in this case it may be equally advantageous to operate upon the lower chord.

Experiments made at Alexandria proved that a timber placed in the position of a main brace, and similarly loaded, was shattered into many pieces, some of which were projected by the force of the explosion more than a hundred feet.

To Render Locomotives unfit for Service: The most expeditious mode is to fire a cannon ball through the boiler. . . .

The Superintendent of the Orange & Alexandria Military RR has instructions to furnish sample torpedoes to officers who may order them. Address "J. H. Devereux, Supt., O&ARR, Alexandria, Virginia."

HERMAN HAUPT

Brig. Gen. Herman Haupt was one of the War's unsung geniuses. A West Pointer, railroad engineer and wooden bridge designer, Haupt in 1862 was engaged in building the Hoosac Tunnel, up in Massachusetts. In April he was called to Washington to become chief of construction and transportation for the United States Military Railroads. He took the job at great personal sacrifice, for his political enemies in Massachusetts were after his funds

and his scalp. In a few short months he succeeded in doing a fine job of building, reconstructing and organizing the scattered rail network under his command.

One of Haupt's first assignments was to rebuild a high bridge on the Richmond, Fredericksburg & Potomac Railroad south of Washington. His product was a trestle—i. e., a bridge supported from the streambed rather than by a truss—which appeared so spidery from a distance that President Lincoln reported to his War Committee:

"That man Haupt has built a bridge across Potomac Creek about 400 feet long and nearly 100 feet high, over which loaded trains are passing every hour, and upon my word, gentle-

*Teamwork and sound construction—not cornstalks—rebuilt this rail crossing into Fredericksburg.*

*A sentry box is the only shelter for troops guarding denuded Chain Bridge against Southern attack.*

men there is nothing in it but beanpoles and cornstalks!"

Haupt used his own patented truss design in several of his military bridges, many of which replaced the less trustworthy trestles. He did not bother to give his wooden bridges permanence by covering them, since he was operating near the battlefront and in territory which might be overrun the next hour by the enemy. Also, wooden sheathing and roofs made tempting marks for guerillas and saboteurs. He saw to it that the Long and Chain Bridges leading across the Potomac into Washington were stripped of their roofs and siding. In this skeleton form they remained until the

end of the War.

The engineer-general recognized the need for still another precaution to take with wooden bridges: he issued orders that troops must break step while marching across a timber span. Many of the old bridges already bore signs announcing Five Dollars Fine for Crossing this Bridge Faster than a Walk, yet the concentrated rhythm of men's feet stepping in unison was a far worse hazard to the trusswork than the clopping trot of horses. Once, near Sharpsburg, Maryland, a military band struck up a thumping tune as a long column of men wound across a valley and through a wooden bridge. An officer realized the danger

*Northern crews, like this one testing an inverted truss, built 26 miles of bridges by War's end.*

and spurred his horse into the middle of the musicians to break up the beat of the tune; by his action he probably saved the bridge from being shaken to pieces.

General Haupt's men used a set procedure and teamwork for erecting a railway bridge truss during the Civil War. There were axemen and teamsters at the rear to prepare and draw timber, framers and raisers at the site to put the bridge together, and a man with a surveyor's instrument to make sure the span was level and straight before a train was run over it.

Haupt left the army after only three months, because of differences with General Pope. A few days later he received a telegram from the War Department. "Come back immediately. Cannot get along without you. Not a wheel moving on any of the roads."

Conscientiously, Haupt returned to bring order out of chaos. He served over a year and then was succeeded by a railroad engineer and bridge designer named Daniel C. McCallum, whom we have already met building patent railway spans for the Erie's lines in Pennsylvania. By the end of the conflict, General McCallum's Railway Construction Corps had ex-

panded from three hundred to ten thousand men, and had built or rebuilt 641 miles of railroad and 26 *miles* of bridges.

On the Confederate side, "Stonewall" Jackson found a man of resource and action to match his own in an elderly Virginia bridge builder named Miles. In retreating, Union soldiers had burned a bridge over the Shenandoah, and Jackson determined to throw to-

*Union Army gang on the Chickahominy in Virginia.*

*Bridge-builders.*

*At-the-scene sketch for Leslie's paper shows fire gaining on Columbia Bridge when a Northern colonel overdid sabotage to halt Rebel advance.*

gether a new span and take after them in a surprise pursuit.

"You put every available man on that bridge," he told old Miles, "and work them all night. It must be ready by daylight. My engineer will give you the plan. You can go right ahead."

At daybreak the next morning General Jackson appeared. "Did the engineer give you the plan for the bridge?" he asked the grizzled old builder.

"General, the bridge is all ready. But to tell the truth," old Miles said, hesitatingly, "I don't know whether that engineer fellow has finished with his picture or not."

One minor episode of war involved the Bendale Bridge just south of Weston, West Virginia. For a while this crossing was the southernmost outpost of the Union lines and was guarded by an Ohio company. A young soldier named William McKinley did picket duty here, while Capt. Rutherford B. Hayes inspected the post. For these two men, both destined for the Presidency, Bendale Bridge offered a welcome shelter.

Robert E. Lee swept into Pennsylvania in June of 1863 with a campaign that was to bring the high tide of the Confederacy to Gettysburg. Harrisburg, other Susquehanna River towns—and even Philadelphia—were trembling with fears of invasion. Squire James Cummings placed a keg of powder in the middle of the Conowingo Bridge over the Susquehanna, and dripped kerosene in a trail to the shore. There he waited to fire the oil and blow up the great spans if a Rebel yell came wafting over the hills from the west.

Farther upstream, between Wrightsville and Columbia, Pennsylvania, stretched that longest covered wooden bridge in the world, 5,620 feet of vulnerable wooden trusswork, roof and siding. This privately owned toll structure carried not only the highway but the Pennsylvania Railroad tracks and a two-level canal towpath. With the Confederates overspreading the valleys to the southwest with their hit-and-run raids, Gen. D. N. Couch, the commander of the Union's Department of the Susquehanna, took possession of the long bridge as a military necessity. A big battle was shaping up and supplies, military stores and troops began to pour across Columbia Bridge in defense of the North.

Sure enough, in a few days a force in gray led by Gen. John B. Gordon appeared and attacked the bridge guards under command of Col. J. G. Frick of the 27th Pennsylvania Volunteers. Colonel Frick beat a prudent retreat back to Columbia across the long bridge and set it afire from end to end with the avowed purpose of "keeping the rebels out of Philadelphia." Checkmated but chivalrous, the Southerners helped put out some fires in Wrightsville that had been started by sparks from the blazing bridge.

Frick's action met with something less than unanimous approval from his own side. The daughter of James Moore, who had built the great bridge some thirty years before, was highly incensed at the destruction. She declared that *she* could have kept the Rebels out of Philadelphia without burning the *whole* mile-long bridge—one span or two would have been enough to do the job! For over forty years the proprietors of the bridge company petitioned Congress for restitution for their loss, but their claims were unsuccessful.

After Gettysburg the fighting took place nearer the heartland of Dixie, where it involved still more covered bridges—some used as forts and prisons. And, as recounted in *Covered Bridges of the Northeast,* a surprise Confederate raid nearly destroyed one at Sheldon, far up near Vermont's Canadian border.

Down in Virginia the final surrender was not far off as the fortunes of war turned in favor of the North. A fugitive slave summed up one of the deciding factors that brought victory. Seeing some of the work of General Haupt's construction gangs, he remarked in awe: "Them Yankees can build bridges quicker than the Rebs can burn 'em down!"

# V

# State by State

So FAR the emphasis has been on the great bridges of the past, and on their historic and engineering significance. Now, in addition, we turn to the covered bridges that are still standing today.

With over thirteen hundred of them to be found in the United States and Canada, they are far from being the nearly-vanished landmarks some accounts would indicate. Pennsylvania is fortunate to be able to claim more covered bridges than any other of the fifty states. According to a recent survey, the Keystone Commonwealth still has 345, nearly a hundred more than Ohio, her closest national competitor. Within the Middle Atlantic area considered in this book, West Virginia is runner-up to Pennsylvania with a number approaching half a hundred. Virginia's total has dwindled to nine, Maryland's to eight, and Delaware clings to just four covered spans.

Thus this region still has more than four hundred covered bridges. They are the heritage from a group that once numbered in the thousands and from a bridge building history going back to 1804. There may be no giants among them, but with their varying types of construction they offer visible evidence of America's progress in civil engineering over the past century and a half.

This chapter tells some of their stories, as well as some tales of their predecessors, and shows where they are to be found.

## DELAWARE: *Brandywine and Red Clay*

DELAWARE, THE NATION'S first state, never had a great many covered bridges. There are records of only about three dozen, and these—including the four still standing—were confined to the northernmost of Delaware's three counties, Newcastle. The rivers of Kent and Sussex Counties are small, marshy and slow-flowing. Uncomplex wooden stringer bridges were adequate for spanning these streams; or, if the crossings were wide, pile-and-trestle causeways were used.

Furthermore, covered bridge annals of Delaware are concerned for the most part with the spans across the Brandywine along its thirteen miles or so from the Pennsylvania border to Wilmington. Local people are proud of the stream's picturesque history. Yet when they wanted a new bridge in the early days they found that it paid off to raise its rank to "river" in their petitions, rather than letting it go as the mere Brandywine Creek that rebels and redcoats bloodied in 1777.

Its setting is as impressive as its legend. An English engineer once described the Brandywine's course as "an amazing country; a succession of large hills, rather sudden, with narrow vales; in short an entire defile."

This defile was the cradle of an industrial empire, and Brandywine water turned wheel after wheel of successive sawmills, gristmills

*Rising Sun mirrored in the Brandywine.*

and, most important, the grinding wheels of the black powder mills of Eleuthère Irénée du Pont de Nemours.

His name, later Americanized to Dupont, indicated that his family once lived near a bridge in France. In his adopted country he could do no less, and his powder mills, strung out along either bank of the tumbling Brandywine, were first cross-joined by small open bridges which gave way to sturdier covered structures as the business grew.

The earliest record of a covered bridge in Delaware is of one built by Lewis Wernwag over the Brandywine "near Wilmington" in 1820–21. This may have been the single-span arch erected near the present Augustine Cut Off a short distance northwest of the city. Other authorities claim Wernwag was the designer of the old Market Street Bridge in the center of Wilmington. This was a double-barreled job, with encased arches, falsefront portals and twin sidewalks, and was a Wilmington landmark down to 1889. Oddly enough, Wern-

wag's is the only name formally recorded as the builder of covered bridges in Delaware, although doubtless an exhaustive search of Newcastle Levy Court minutes would turn up others.

Near Dupont's center of operations was Rising Sun, a powder-keg mill and cluster of workers' homes with another twin-lane span high above the Brandywine. This bridge, built in 1833, had a useful life of well over eighty years. Farther upstream were Rockland and Thompson's Bridges, which survived until recent times.

The most unusual of Delaware's thirty-odd covered bridges crossed the famed Deep Cut of the Chesapeake & Delaware Canal. Twenty-five hundred men dug and blasted through a ridge of solid rock nearly a mile long to create

*Its husky arch and kingposts fostered belief that Wernwag designed Wilmington's Market St. Bridge.*

*This picture, c. 1870, shows the beginning of the end for Summit Bridge, high over the Deep Cut.*

this gash. Even before the canal was complete, the man-made chasm was spanned in 1825 by a graceful wooden arch some 90 feet above the water. This covered bridge, with its ornate windows and boxed portals, became a landmark to helmsmen guiding their canal boats behind plodding mules along the old waterway. Known as both Buck's Bridge and Sum-

mit Bridge, the high span was replaced in 1872 by a swing drawbridge at a lower level.

The four covered bridges that still stand in Delaware are all confined to an area within a six-mile radius south of the state's curved northern boundary. Located among parklike fields between the hills, the four can be found in an hour by a careful driver armed with a

*Why cover bridges?—Wooddale span, left, is tight and strong, the one upstream is doomed.*

*Neat Ashland Mill Bridge on Red Clay Creek.*

good map and a sense of direction.

Slightly north of the Lancaster Pike is Wooddale, the site of the first of three remaining covered spans over Red Clay Creek. The other two are upstream on either side of the little village of Ashland. All three Red Clay bridges are of Town lattice construction, and it is pretty obvious that they were built about the same time by the same builder or builders.

The Wooddale Bridge is tight to the road, and its trusses were purposely built on a slight skew to fit the angle of the abutments. It serves only a single home. Also on a skew is the abandoned bridge below Ashland. This span is in ruinously poor condition, not having been used in thirty years, but its battered framework still manages to keep from sagging into Red Clay Creek.

West of Ashland a tree- and fence-lined road leads across the third bridge, which has been made part and parcel with its surroundings by dint of green portals and sides painted gray. Those who maintained these bridges have had highly individual ideas about how they should be painted. Wooddale has its faded portal panels outlined in red, the one west of Ashland once was a gleaming white,

and the weary skeleton south of Ashland bears unmistakable signs of having been painted an eye-knocking red and yellow!

Northeast of Granogue, and only a few paces from the arc of the northern boundary, is Smith's Bridge, the finest and best-preserved covered bridge in Delaware. Built in 1839 at at a cost of $5,446, this 154-foot bridge with its concentric arches carries a good deal of traffic across Brandywine Creek. Smith's Bridge was completely overhauled in 1955—re-sided, re-roofed and repainted. It is red with white trim now, instead of the original weatherworn white lead and interior whitewash. For added safety two new piers were placed in the Brandywine below the old structure. The grind and roar of the powder mills is long gone from the Brandywine, but Smith's Bridge over its fabled waters still gives the stream an aura of days gone by.

*Sturdy reminder of Brandywine legends: arched Smith's Bridge at Granogue is Delaware's finest.*

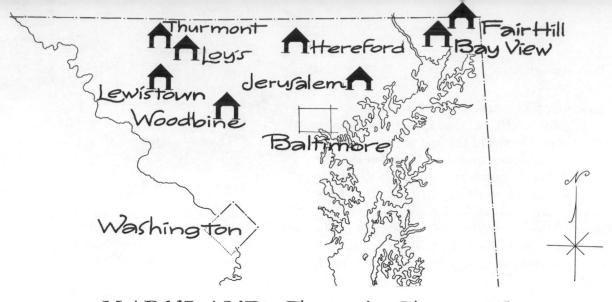

Thurmont  
Loys  
Hereford  
Fair Hill  
Bay View  
Jerusalem  
Lewistown  
Woodbine  
Baltimore  
Washington  
N

# *MARYLAND: Terrapin Trusswork*

MARYLAND WAS IN THE forefront of wooden bridge development. In addition to having the first covered wooden overpass and the first wooden truss railroad spans, the Old Line State had its share of highway bridges, big and little.

The biggest covered bridges in Maryland were the first to be built. The Susquehanna was a formidable barrier interrupting the lines of commerce between Baltimore and Philadelphia. True, ferries operated across the wide reaches extending from the river's mouth; but they were poky—and downright dangerous when ice choked the channels.

Maryland promoters had two sites in mind for toll bridges and, prompted by the success of the Pennsylvania companies upstream, pushed through their charters in the legislature. The first was planned to island-hop across the Susquehanna at Rock Run, just above Port Deposit. The company asked Theodore Burr down from Harrisburg to build it. Even though he was already engaged in spanning the mighty river at three other spots, Burr eagerly took on the contract for this one. He just couldn't resist the temptation.

In 1817 the famous builder started on the 4,170-foot bridge at Rock Run. It had eighteen arch spans, each 200 feet long; used stretches of three beautiful islands as extended piers, and stood nearly 26 feet above the water.

As usual, Burr was frequently absent from the job, off upriver to look after his other bridges. The Reverend Mr. Magraw, the local Presbyterian minister, had ideas on how the Rock Run bridge should be built and didn't hesitate to state them. He gave free advice on the erection of heavy timbers, and noised it around that Theodore Burr was not only getting paid for work he wasn't doing, but the contractor was hitting the bottle.

Burr got wind of this backbiting and retaliated. One morning Port Deposit awoke to find handbills plastered on every tree. "The Rev. Theodore Burr," the placards said, "will preach a sermon on the wooded island in the Susquehanna River, reached by a portion of his new and elegant bridge at Rock Run." The date was the following Sunday.

Curious raftsmen, farmers and tradespeople turned out in droves to crowd the pleasant little island and hear Mr. Burr. All agreed that he preached a right tolerable sermon—presumably on the virtues of minding one's own business. Mr. Magraw's church was practically empty. Come Tuesday, having simmered down, the minister sued for peace. Thereafter the Reverend tended to saving souls and Theodore Burr to building bridges.

Seven miles upstream Lewis Wernwag had settled down awhile to run a sawmill at Conowingo. Here another company had a Maryland

44

*Gaunt wooden arches competed with steel in Conowingo Crossing, above, shortly before the ten-span mongrel was blown to bits; below, the Susquehanna giant in its heyday.*

charter for a Susquehanna bridge, and the German-born builder was a natural to plan and erect it. Although he began a year later, Wernwag completed his ten-span, 1,744-foot Conowingo Bridge about the same time as Burr finished his elegant Rock Run crossing. The rivalry between builders was taken up by the companies who stood to make money on tollgathering. All up and down Maryland's Harford Pike and the great Street Road leading from Philadelphia were posters in big letters: CROSS SUSQUEHANNA BY ROCK RUN BRIDGE! or, USE CONOWINGO CROSSING!

Both bridges were beset with troubles. In January, 1823, shortly after Burr's untimely death, an ironshod sleigh was being dragged through Rock Run Bridge toward Port Deposit. It scraped and squealed on the dry floor, and the nailheads sent out such prodigious sparks that some wisps of hay ignited. The whole eastern half of the bridge went up in flames.

Lewis Wernwag floated timber down from Conowingo and rebuilt Rock Run. Over the years the crossing lost its popularity and the bridge became dilapidated. In 1854 a herd of a hundred and thirty-six cattle was being driven across the quaking roadway. Suddenly those in the lead shied at flickers of light glinting off the river below. Bellowing, they stam-

*This rare canal bridge stood near Cumberland.*

peded back upon the others, and in the melee two bridge spans collapsed. Salvagers in Port Deposit had fresh beef for supper that night. The bridge was not repaired, and three years later a great ice gorge swept it away. Today only stumpy rock piles in the Susquehanna mark the site of Maryland's longest covered bridge, which contained arches fashioned by two of America's greatest pioneer bridge designers.

Rock Run had nearly been destroyed in 1846 when the whole ten spans of Conowingo Bridge came down in a freshet. By some miracle the wreckage snagged or broke up before it reached Port Deposit. A second covered bridge at Conowingo survived a series of fires and ice jams, and sections of it were gradually replaced by steel. Two of the old wooden spans were still in place when the bridge was dynamited out of existence in 1927. U.S. 1 now crosses the Susquehanna River on top of the

hydroelectric dam three miles downstream.

The spread of covered bridges in Maryland seems to have been contained in an area of the northern and central counties which was crossed by the great travel routes. Tidewater counties and the Eastern Shore relied upon short spans and trestle-piling to cross their shallow rivers.

The elongated western neck of the state was, in addition to being wooded, also good limestone country, and its population included many stonemasons. So, instead of erecting covered wooden spans, the western Marylander built what he considered more permanent structures: stone bridges. It took masons much longer to erect their crossings and the expense was a vast drain on local pocketbooks. However, in fairness it must be said that many of the old stone bridges still span the creeks and rivers of this section of the state, standing over streams with mouth-filling names like Conococheague and Youghiogheny.

The famed Cumberland Road (now U.S. 40) used stone bridges on its western sections. But covered wooden bridges were relied upon to take this great highway of western expansion high and dry above the Catoctin near Middletown, the Monocacy at Bridgeport and the Patapsco in Ellicott City. The Jefferson and Buckeystown Pikes out of Frederick had them, too.

One very unusual covered bridge used to stand right in the heart of Baltimore. This was old Belvedere Bridge, which crossed Jones Falls at a point near the present entrance to Greenmount Cemetery. Here a main artery of travel once entered the city from the northeast, and the crossing called for a sizable bridge. George Milliman built it in 1820, probably on a plan furnished by Lewis Wernwag after The Colossus became famous. No bridge exactly like the Belvedere had ever been seen before, and no beholder seems to have attempted to duplicate it anywhere in America. The level roadway hung between two concentric arches, crisscrossed by iron rod

**The Thrill That Comes Once in a Lifetime --**    By H. T. Webster

10¢ FINE FOR DRIVING OVER THIS BRIDGE FASTER THAN A WALK

NOW, ELMER!

WE GOT ALONG FAIRLY WELL IN THE NINETIES WITHOUT THE AMUSEMENT PARKS' TUNNEL OF LOVE

   11-30-

*Paraphrasing The Colossus made Belvedere strong, but the Baltimore spans were never copied.*

bracing and extra internal arches. Odd but practical, Belvedere Bridge served Baltimore for over six decades.

Under the whiplash of storm, attacked by fire and obliterated by the sometimes misguided hand of Progress, Maryland's covered bridges have gradually disappeared from the landscape. Twenty years ago there were seventeen, but today the total is down to eight.

Frederick County has the most and best of the lot. In an isolated rural setting, the Roddy Bridge northeast of Thurmont is most attractive. Only 40 feet long, this red-painted structure seems right at home over Owens Creek. Loy's Bridge serves a busier road downstream to the east; with high trusses and horizontal siding, its gaunt bulk looms up to startle a stranger traveling by night.

The third Frederick County bridge began its existence as a crossing of the Monocacy River. A summer flood in 1889 lifted the span gently from its abutments and deposited it upright and intact on the bank a few rods below. For some obscure reason, instead of being reset in its original location the bridge was dismantled and carted some three miles west. There, piece by piece, the framework and arches were re-erected at Utica Mills over

Fishing Creek. Timbers with unused notches still can be found in its dim interior, attesting to the fact that the rebuilder simply "made do" when he ran out of matched pieces. In recent years this migrant covered bridge has been strengthened with an additional center pier and painted a deep red to harmonize with the landscape.

Gunpowder Falls in Baltimore County once had covered bridges at Monkton and Loch Raven. Only one, Bunker Hill Bridge, spans this stream today. It stands on a side road northwest of Hereford. Built in 1880 and restored in 1947, it has an arch-truss after Theodore Burr's design and overhanging portals that sport a neat board-and-batten finish.

On the Harford County line in the hinterland between the heavy traffic on U.S. 1 and U.S. 40, Little Gunpowder Falls is crossed at Jerusalem by a similar Burr arch bridge. It, too, has been restored in recent years. Hervey Brackbill of the *Baltimore Sun,* interviewing an elderly gentleman at Jerusalem, happened to ask if the span had any ghosts.

"Yes," was the gruff reply. "Parkers!"

"Parkers?" Brackbill smelled a story. "Who was Parker and what did he do?"

"Parkers!" came the retort. "Young fellers

and girls. They drive in the bridge at night and park!"

The youth of Maryland, using modern conveyances, was still living up to the old romantic traditions of the state's covered bridges.

Over near Abington, careless "parkers" were probably responsible for the passing of one of Maryland's most attractive roofed spans. Nobody saw the lonely little bridge over Bynum Run go. It just burned on a hot July night in 1955, and the ashes weren't discovered until morning.

Cecil County, in Maryland's northeast corner, once vied with Frederick for the distinction of having the greatest number of covered bridges. In addition to the mammoth Susquehanna crossings, there were nearly a dozen over Big and Little Elk and Northeast Creeks. These included tiny Kirks and Reynolds Bridges just south of Blue Ball—they were once described with scorn as "just oversized dog kennels with two ends"—and Foster's Bridge northeast of Fairview which perched virtually across the Mason-Dixon Line. Parks' Rolling Mill Bridge and Scott's Bridge near Cowenton were abandoned and collapsed from neglect.

One of two covered bridges remaining in Cecil County, the tottering relic over Northeast Creek at Bayview, is an example of what good intentions with no cash backing can accomplish. Built about 1860, it was a well-made Burr arch of one span, and bridged the creek at a scenic spot called Gilpin's Rocks.

In the 1930's State Route 272 was laid out to use this crossing at a new site adjacent to the old bridge, which was to be demolished. Little was heard locally until a civic group from Salisbury announced they would like to have the bridge. Their intention was to move it to a park in their Eastern Shore city. It would be a fine tourist attraction.

"Well!" snorted Bayviewers. "It's *our* bridge and *our* attraction. Let's keep it right here!"

The state complied and the bridge was left intact, floating in a limbo between jurisdictions where nobody was officially responsible for its continued existence. For a while a neighboring farmer stored hay in it. Little by little Gilpin's Rocks Bridge deteriorated: a shingle loose, a board off; then the quiet drip, drip, drip of rain to turn the exposed wood to punk. In the heavy snows of early 1958 the roof collapsed. A year later the bridge had outlasted its concrete successor, but only as a skeletonized ruin. It's probably far too late to take it to Salisbury now.

On the brighter side of the picture is Cecil County's best-kept bridge, standing over Big Elk Creek to the northwest of Appleton. For miles the fields and woods here are part of William Dupont's vast Foxcatcher Farms, and the bridge, once public, now serves a private road on the estate. Well maintained and painted a brilliant red with white trim, Foxcatcher Farms Bridge should continue to be a fine example of Maryland's covered bridges for years to come.

*Wartime sketch of former Potomac bridge to Leesburg, Va., after it was taken by Union troops.*

Burr truss, good care promise long life for Bunker Hill.

Bayview before its roof collapsed.

Span over Big Elk Creek is the pride of Foxcatcher Farms.

Jerusalem's old-fashioned spirit is catching; below, Roddy Bridge.

Loy's Bridge stands over Owens Creek.

Swapped timbers rebuilt Utica Mills.

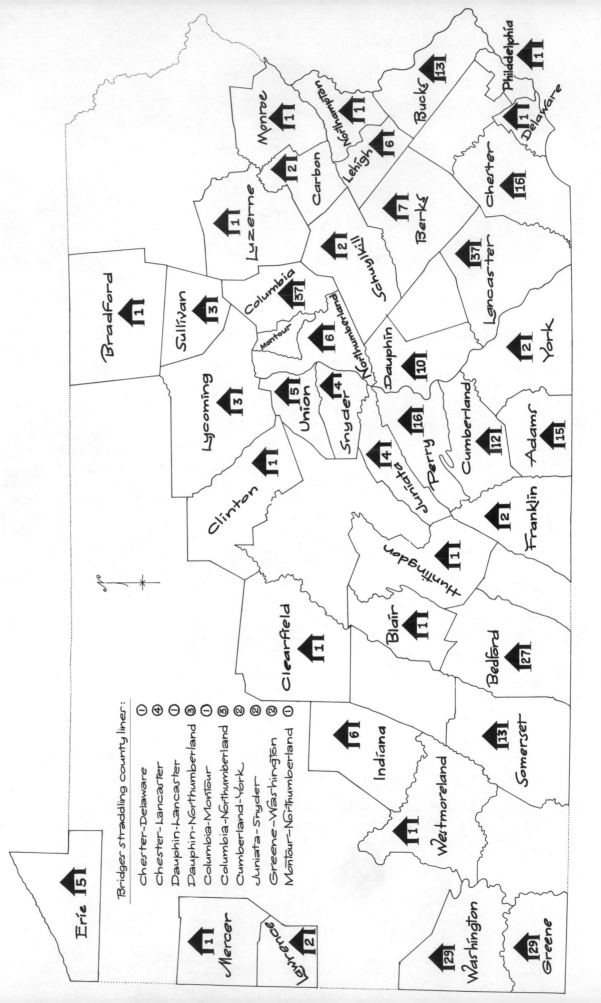

Erie **5**

Mercer **1**

Lawrence **2**

Bradford **1**

Sullivan **3**

Monroe **1**

Luzerne **2**

Northampton **1**

Lehigh **6**

Carbon

Bucks **13**

Philadelphia **1**

Delaware **1**

Chester **16**

Berks **7**

Schuylkill **2**

Columbia **37**

Montour

Northumberland **6**

Lancaster **37**

Lycoming **3**

Union **5**

Snyder **4**

Dauphin **10**

York **2**

Clinton **1**

Juniata **4**

Perry **16**

Cumberland **12**

Adams **15**

Clearfield **1**

Blair **1**

Huntingdon **1**

Franklin **2**

Bedford **27**

Indiana **6**

Westmoreland **1**

Somerset **13**

Washington **29**

Greene **29**

Bridges straddling county lines:

- Chester-Delaware — ①
- Chester-Lancaster — ④
- Dauphin-Lancaster — ①
- Dauphin-Northumberland — ③
- Columbia-Montour — ①
- Columbia-Northumberland — ③
- Cumberland-York — ②
- Juniata-Snyder — ②
- Greene-Washington — ②
- Montour-Northumberland — ①

# PENNSYLVANIA:
## Keystone of American Bridge Building

RUDYARD KIPLING ONCE WROTE that a Pennsylvania morning held, with the immortal earth, the things that really last beyond men and time. His words can well be applied to the Commonwealth's covered bridges. In numbers, with between three and four hundred existing roofed spans, the state leads any of the other fifty by a sizable margin. Heaven knows how many Pennsylvania must have had in the past: hazarding a guess, at least fifteen hundred—more than all that stand in the entire United States today.

Yet it's not sheer multitude alone that makes the Keystone bridges so valuable to historians and engineers. The state had not only the nation's first known covered bridge, but also has some of the latest to be erected; one private timbered crossing was built as recently as 1956. With its many unique structures and its large and old spans in so many areas, Pennsylvania is tops for covered bridges.

Records show that all but three of the state's sixty-seven counties had covered spans. Even at this writing there are three hundred and forty-five bridges scattered over forty of them. The greatest concentration is shared equally by Columbia and Lancaster Counties with thirty-seven apiece. In describing the whereabouts of the Commonwealth's present and past landmarks, though, it seems logical to group the bridges according to watersheds to start with—those of the Delaware, Susquehanna, Ohio Valley, Potomac and Lake Erie—and then break down these major divisions according to the counties through which the great streams and their tributaries flow. The large number of existing covered spans also dictates five separate maps for clarity's sake.

## THE DELAWARE WATERSHED

The Delaware River winds generally southward from the Catskill foothills to the Bay, and at one time was spanned by no less than twenty-one interstate covered bridges. All but the railroad bridge at Easton were built originally by companies interested in the tolls that could be collected. This wide river barrier to trade with New Jersey was bound to attract the attention of the earliest builders of covered bridges: our three top bridge architects put their arch and trusswork fabrications across the Delaware.

Theodore Burr led the parade. On January 30, 1806, his immense bridge between Morrisville and Trenton was opened for business. This was the second covered bridge ever built in America, and the first between two states. The 1008-foot, five-arch crossing was one of Burr's experimental jobs, with the roadway

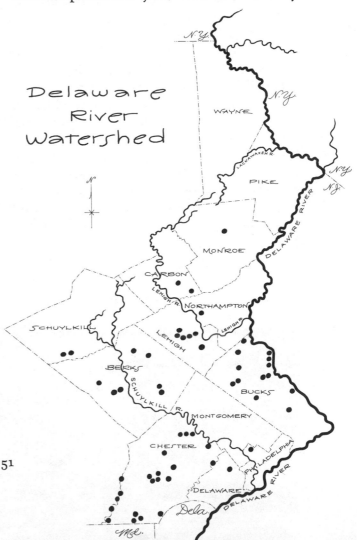

*Splendid Burr arches made Morrisville's interstate crossing one of the world's finest bridges.*

hung directly from the huge arches. In later years it became a railroad bridge, too, as part of the Pennsylvania's main line.

Timothy Palmer's tightly enclosed bridge at Easton was completed only a few months after Burr's and was the only bridge that the New-buryport designer built with a level roadway. At New Hope, between the first two giants, Lewis Wernwag threw *his* carefully planned crossing over the Delaware in 1814. It was a six-span, 1050-foot affair into whose trusses he put more iron bracing than had ever been used before by bridge builders.

In general, the Delaware River was not the scene of jurisdictional squabbles such as plagued other boundary rivers between states. To begin with, its bridges were owned by private companies. If the boundary question was considered at all during covered bridge days, the crossings were thought of as being in whichever state—Pennsylvania, New Jersey or New York—where its individual users resided.

"I didn't dare cross over to Lambertville," recalls an old resident of New Hope after he had shot off some premature fireworks in the Jersey town. "The sheriff would have nabbed me the minute I stepped off the bridge."

In response to a growing agitation for free bridges, over the years the toll companies on the York State border sold out their interests to the adjoining states. The Delaware River Joint Toll Bridge Commission, formed in 1913, gradually took over those between Pennsylvania and New Jersey, and now maintains and operates the modern successors to the old covered bridges on a fifty-fifty basis of cost apportionment between the two states.

Although suspension wire cable spans were the favorite means of crossing the upper Delaware, Pennsylvania was once joined to New York by covered bridges at Long Eddy, Cochecton, Narrowsburg and Matamoras.

Narrowsburg, aptly named, was the site of two successive ones. The first, a 184-foot single-span Town lattice, was described as "a monstrous bridge, but no more so than the monstrous tolls for traversing it." A 262-foot job took its place in 1859. It was a Long-type truss with special auxiliary arches devised by the builder, George W. Thayer of Springfield, Massachusetts. Whether the tolls were increased with its length is not recorded.

*Progress—not 90 years of ice like this—decreed the end of Palmer's great bridge at Easton.*

*Narrowsburg was lucky for raftsmen and tollgatherers from 1859 to 1899.*

Raftsmen, skillfully piloting their cumbersome loads of lumber down the Delaware to Philadelphia, knew and hated all the bridges. The pierless Narrowsburg Bridge over its deep pool was an exception. Passing below, the rafters made a ritual of trying to toss their hats into the crisscrossed beams under the floor. If a hat stuck, the flotilla would be assured a safe voyage to Philly. If not—well, rafting was a chancy business anyhow.

At the last bend which divides Pennsylvania from New York, the notorious Gould-Fisk "gang" of the Erie Railroad once pulled off a smooth bit of chicanery. In consideration for being allowed to lay their rails on the Pennsylvania side farther up the Delaware, the Erie managers had agreed to connect their boom town of Port Jervis, New York, to Matamoras with a covered bridge, and "maintain said bridge forever."

The bridge was built in 1852, and much commotion was stirred up to have the Erie bring a branch line over the span and on down to Milford, Pennsylvania. This the railroad company apparently had no intention of doing. A March wind in 1870 wrecked the bridge, and the Erie solemnly declared that all rights in the crossing had been sold to the Lamonte Mining & RR Co., who would shortly rebuild. Nothing happened. At last a Pike County legislator thought to check the "Lamonte" charter in Harrisburg. Not a one of the incorporators could be identified: their names were all fictitious. And Matamoras stayed bridgeless for years and never did get a railroad.

In addition to financing the experimental designs of Burr, Palmer and Wernwag, the backers of the Delaware River toll bridges put up money to prove the worth of several other types. Peleg Kingsley, down from North-

*Insatiable river gnaws at Riverton-Belvidere bridge in flood that crippled eight Delaware giants.*

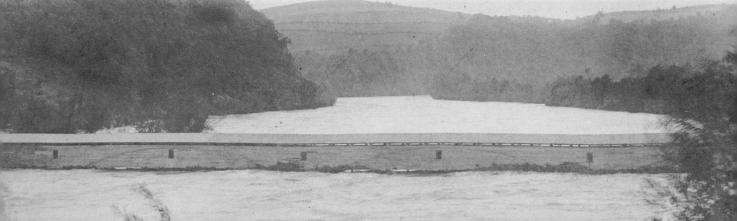

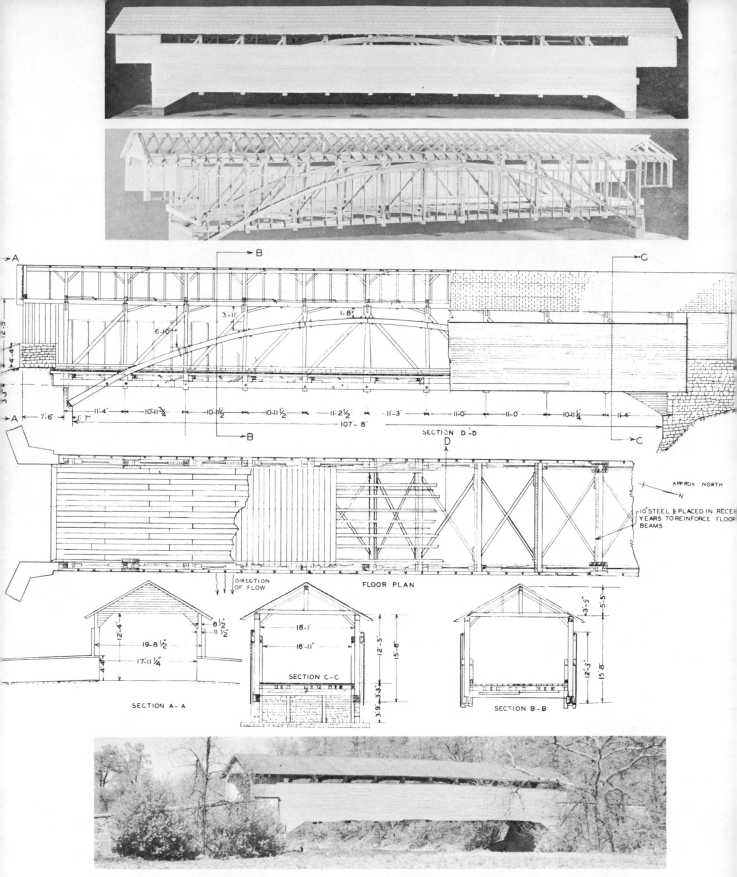

*Typical of eastern Pennsylvania: Manassas Guth Bridge in model, blueprint and finished form.*

ampton, Massachusetts, built the first Centre Bridge, using long open arches which were eventually covered. Solon Chapin of Easton was equally proficient at building either Town lattice or the regionally more popular Burr-type bridges, and he was responsible for the Delaware crossings at Riverton, Riegelsville and Lumberville. The last covered bridge to be erected on the interstate border went up in 1869, connecting Portland, Pennsylvania, with Columbia, New Jersey. This was the work of Charles Kellogg of Athens, Pennsylvania, a professional engineer who later headed his own iron bridge building company.

Some Delaware River toll companies were unlucky in their choice of unnamed builders. A bridge one outfit built at Milford—the town denied a spur line by the Erie—was too low and washed away twice. Two timber replacements on the same site both fell of their own weight. The great flood of 1841 tore out eight covered crossings of the lower Delaware, including Lewis Wernwag's pride, the New Hope Bridge. Nearly the same thing happened in 1903 when another eight were either swept away completely or lost a span or two. Only Centre Bridge, which Amos Campbell had rebuilt with a lattice truss and raised a careful six feet higher after the '41 debacle, stood intact between Easton and Trenton. Upper Black Eddy lost a span, but it was replaced in kind with timber salvaged from the flood-wrecked Riegelsville bridge upriver. Uhlertown and Lumberville were patched up with new iron spans.

One by one the flood survivors were rebuilt in steel and concrete by the Delaware River Joint Toll Bridge Commission, and valley residents felt that they were losing old friends. The river's last covered bridge stood at Portland for eighty-six years. At the time of its destruction by the floodwaters of 1955, this four-span bridge, 760 feet from bank to bank, was the longest in the United States.

Only a handful of covered bridges are known to have stood in northeastern Pennsyl-

*Sturdy Little Gap span on Princess Creek.*

vania. The lumber regions appear to have shipped their timbers to city markets rather than use them locally in building wooden bridges. One covered span over the Lackawaxen River at Honesdale is remembered for the tornado that lifted it bodily off its abutments and sent the roof soaring high over town. Despite a battering by high water in 1955, Carbon County clings to two photogenic bridges: one at Little Gap across Princess Creek, and another east of Harrity over the Pohopoco.

The Lehigh, flowing down from the coal country past Allentown and Bethlehem, was another proving ground for early bridge builders. Long covered structures which survived into the present century were at Cementon, Coplay, Bethlehem and Glendon.

Today, Lehigh County has five well-preserved covered bridges on side roads over Jordan Creek northwest of Allentown. Here we first encounter the "trademarks" of the typical eastern Pennsylvania covered bridge: high stone parapet approaches, sturdy matched timbers and coats of paint on horizontal siding. The bridges go by local names which serve to identify them even better than geographical directions from nearby towns. Those in Lehigh are called Geiger's, Rex's, Wehr's, Schlicher's and Manassas Guth. A sixth bridge, Bogert's,

*Bethlehem's former Lehigh River Bridge.*

Bucks spans include Knecht's above, Sundale, right.

And Van Sandt on Pidcock Creek; Pine Valley, below.

And Houpt's Mill, left, and Sheard's Mill, right.

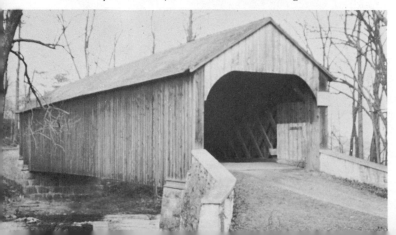

stands just south of the city of Allentown, preserved in Lehigh Parkway. Twice doomed in recent years, articles in local newspapers brought about eventual state aid and renovation for this span. The Save the Bogert's Bridge Committee was pictured in cartoons as a militant group defending the structure with a cannon. Actually, a letter-writing campaign did the trick.

Bucks County has avid supporters of covered bridges, too. In 1958 determined effort and a money-raising drive not only saved the South Perkasie Bridge, built in 1832, but moved it intact to a new site in Lenape Park. The oldest covered bridge in the county, Perkasie sports a faded injunction on its portals which never fails to delight tourists:

$5 FINE FOR ANY PERSON RIDING OR DRIVING
OVER THIS BRIDGE FASTER THAN A WALK OR
SMOKING SEGARS ON

This county is a notable exception to the general Pennsylvanian preference for Burr arch bridges. Every one of the thirteen covered bridges scattered about the old/new Bucks County countryside use Mr. Ithiel Town's lattice truss. Most likely this local favoritism stems from Amos Campbell's early introduction of the lattice in his Delaware River crossings nearby. Bucks County builders came and admired, and then went back to build likewise over such creeks as Tinicum, Tohickon and Perkiomen. Nine of the spans date from 1871–76, and most were the work of local builders, G. Arnst, P. S. Naylor and David Sutton.

Bucks numbers among its landmarks the only covered bridge in the East which crosses a canal. This 101-foot crossing is just below an old lock of the Delaware Canal at Uhlertown, back in from the Delaware River under a high bluff. Fifty years ago two canalers, Shinn and Copp, were sparking the same Riegelsville barmaid. When she finally picked Copp as the lucky fellow, "Captain" Shinn was furious. One evening as he tied up below the store at Uhlertown, Shinn spied his rival's barge being locked through above. He hurried to the bridge and crawled out through the lattices. As the mules passed along the towpath and the boat glided under him, "Cap" pounced down in the gloom upon the unsuspecting helmsman.

A quick scuffle showed Shinn he had the right boat but the wrong man. His erstwhile friend had hired a brawny Irishman from Mauch Chunk to run the boat while he was away on his honeymoon. Shinn took two rights and a left before soaring off in a graceful arc to land in the muddy canal.

The broad Schuylkill was once spanned by close to forty covered highway and railroad bridges, from Tamaqua in the anthracite region to Gray's Ferry near its mouth. There were a dozen road crossings in Berks County alone, with the first one erected on Penn Street in Reading back in 1818. This pioneer effort, a Lewis Wernwag–Isaac Nathans collaboration, was long the pride of Reading. The proprietors even had sculptor William Rush come up from Philadelphia to duplicate for its wide portals the ornamental wooden figures of Agriculture and Commerce with which he had adorned the Permanent Bridge some twelve years before. For decades the youth of Reading admired the

lush form of Agriculture as she reclined, full-blown, on a wagonload of golden wheat.

Also over the Schuylkill was the double-barreled bridge at Hamburg whose portals were enhanced with Corinthian columns in the style of Wernwag's Colossus; it even had lightning rods for extra protection from storms. This one stood until 1928, exactly a century.

Another unique Berks County bridge was the one at Stoudt's Ferry, built in 1857 to the northwest of Reading. The bridge over the Schuylkill at that particular point had two functions, one routine and the other seemingly impossible to fulfill: it had to carry a highway, but it also had to carry across two towpaths serving the up- and downstream boat traffic of the Schuylkill Canal, which changed sides at Stoudt's Ferry to continue on its way. The problem was aggravated by the fact that the walks over which the mules crossed in opposite directions (depending upon whether they were hauling cargo up or down the river) had to be arranged so that the towlines would not foul each other.

The problem was solved with an ingenious system which anticipated today's cloverleaf traffic intersections by almost a hundred years. The diagram shows the inspired common sense of the solution. The sidewalks for mules were supported only from below, and were protected by a wide cantilevered roof. The ends of each walk ended in a stone-walled circular ramp which allowed the patient mules to double back on themselves briefly after leaving the bridge, and continue their boat's course without once snagging their towlines. Outermost were the rounded guide railings over which the taut lines passed, with a minimum of friction, to the snub-nosed barges moving athwart the current below.

Stoudt's Ferry enjoyed another distinction. For many years it was the world's longest single-span covered bridge in existence. Partisans in Switzerland, New York State and California made loud their claims to the honor, but unsung Stoudt's Ferry was really it. Although it

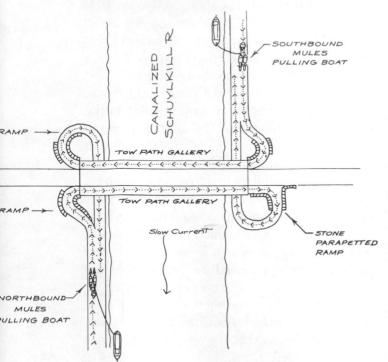

Labels on diagram:
SOUTHBOUND MULES PULLING BOAT
CANALIZED SCHUYLKILL R.
RAMP
TOW PATH GALLERY
TOW PATH GALLERY
Slow Current
STONE PARAPETTED RAMP
NORTHBOUND MULES PULLING BOAT
RAMP

*From a distance Stoudt's Ferry span, above, gave little hint of complex traffic controls at left.*

there are only seven. The oldest is Greismer's Mill Bridge at Spangsville, erected in 1832. Close by at Pleasantville is another covered bridge, built on the customary Burr plan but unusual in that the arches are down below the housing of the roadway. Red-painted Dreibelbis Bridge, south of Lenhartsville over Maiden Creek, is another Berks landmark.

*Pleasantville's strong-bellied underarch.*

was no rival to Burr's short-lived McCall's Ferry Bridge, its immense arched trusses had a clear span of 238 feet—totaling 28 feet longer than the nearest claimant; and another 45 feet could be added if you counted the overhang at each portal. It's a pity that no known record gives the name of the designer-builder of Stoudt's Ferry Bridge.

On September 12, 1948, the great bridge, long a victim of neglect, gave up the fight and collapsed with a shriek of protesting timbers into the Schuylkill. Thereafter the 210-foot Blenheim Bridge in York State could rightly claim the title it had long been advertising, that of being the "longest single-span covered bridge in the world."

Thirty-seven covered bridges were built in Berks County between 1818 and 1887. Today

Bushong's, a 330-foot two-spanner over the mouth of Tulpehocken Creek opposite Reading was, until its destruction by fire in March of 1959, Pennsylvania's second longest covered bridge. Two more over Tulpehocken are within walking distance of Reading. One is Van Reed's Paper Mill Bridge, far past the century mark in age. The other, a comparative youngster erected in 1867, goes by the name of Red Bridge—although for years and years it has been painted white! Just a trifle under 200 feet in length, it is Pennsylvania's longest single-span covered bridge.

Norristown, in Montgomery County, once had a big bridge over the Schuylkill with the unusual feature of three lanes, two for vehicles

*Dreibelbis Bridge south of Lenhartsville.*

*Montgomery County's Red Hill span.*

and a center path for pedestrians. It burned in 1924. The county's other prominent covered structure, near Red Hill, survived until 1955. This 300-foot, four-span job of lattice truss-work over a wide reach of Perkiomen Creek was still usable and in good repair when it was doomed by the building of a new water supply reservoir.

By crossing the Schuylkill to Chester County you can find some sixteen covered bridges, survivors of a number which once reached over a hundred. They are well kept for the most part, and blend with the Chester landscape of farms, woodlots and roads so old that constant use has lowered their levels below those of the surrounding fields.

Some of this county's bridges are red, some white and two are painted yellow. All open out on the typical stone abutments called "Pennsylvania parapets." They enjoy the pleasing distinction of usually going by the names of local people once associated with them, rather than by more impersonal geographic designations. The name of at least one Chester County builder survives because of this friendly practice. Alex Kennedy put up a neat yellow-painted span over French Creek north of Kimberton in 1856, assisted by Jesse King. More than a century later he is still given everyday credit for his handiwork. "Did you come by Rapp's?" a farmer will inquire, "or by Kennedy's?"

The white Knox Bridge at the edge of Valley Forge State Park is the best-known span in the county. Although some farfetched tales have General Washington praying for victory beside this bridge, the plain fact is that it was built in 1865 to replace an all-stone structure wrecked by flood. Knox Bridge may well have been recorded on more film than any other covered span in the Keystone State, thanks to its location near a top tourist attraction. A visiting Britisher, snapping it in color, asked innocently:

"Why did they cover the old fellow? Was it for protection against the Red Indians?"

*No Washington, no redskins for Knox Bridge.*

A few years ago Chester County claimed the nation's oldest covered bridge. It was Marshall's, spanning the Brandywine at Northbrook, with its erection date given as 1807. Undoubtedly it was an old bridge, but it was built precisely on the patent design Theodore Burr took out, up in York State only three years before. It seems unlikely that this plan could have filtered down into rural Pennsylvania quite so soon, especially since Burr did not move into the state to begin his Susquehanna giants until 1812. More probably, this bridge was the replacement for an earlier structure whose date

*Hall's Bridge on French Creek in Chester County.*

*Burr arches say something special to many a bridge buff, and Glen Hall's have replaced iron spans.*

was transferred to the new span. Whatever claims Marshall's had were wiped out in November, 1953, when the Pennsylvania Highway Department unceremoniously cut its white pine arches and let it drop into the Brandywine.

Upstream at Glen Hall there is another Burr-type span which in 1881 had the distinction of replacing an unsafe iron bridge. For their sheer beauty of setting a visitor should also see Speakman's and Hayes-Clark Bridges, close together over Buck and Doe Runs on the King Ranch property south of Coatesville, or the out-of-the-way McCreery's Bridge over Black Run, tucked away in the Octoraro Valley to the southwest. In addition to its sixteen, Chester shares four covered bridges with its western neighbor, Lancaster County.

From Chester, too, a bridge, now by-passed, crosses eastward into Delaware County only a short commuter's hop from Philadelphia. This is Bartram's Bridge over Crum Creek, west of Newtown Square. The portal sheathing on

*Note parapets for two-county Bellbank Bridge.*

Bartram's is unique, and its arch carries the barely legible inscription:

Lincoln—Save Union and the Congress

An odd-looking covered bridge once stood over Crum Creek a few miles downstream. It served the old Leiper Quarry, which was reached by both an access highway and one of the earliest industrial railroads ever built. The wide two-lane bridge served both road and rails for many years, but with the advent of heavier rolling stock the railroad portion was neatly sliced off and replaced by girders beneath the track. The highway part carried on perfectly well after the amputation.

*Leiper Quarry Bridge is half a double-barrel.*

The great Schuylkill covered bridges which brought commerce and fame to Philadelphia disappeared many years ago. Lewis Wernwag's mighty Colossus, described by actress Fanny Kemble as "a white scarf, thrown across the water," was the first to go. It was burned accidentally on the evening of September 1, 1838, and as many people lined the Schuylkill's banks to watch its passing as had witnessed its first crucial test a quarter of a century before. Burned, as well, was Dan'l Stone's Market Street Bridge (replacing Palmer's Permanent Bridge) which departed in a spectacular blaze on November 20, 1875. The Philadelphia, Wilmington & Baltimore Railroad quietly replaced its latticed Newkirk Viaduct at Gray's Ferry; and in 1886 it came the turn of the Columbia Railroad Bridge at Peters' Island to be razed.

Wissahickon Creek, northwest of Philadelphia, is a famous little stream whose water power once turned the wheels of nearly sixty mills. In the old days the winding stream was spanned by at least six covered bridges, which went by distinctive names like "Old Red," "Livezey's," and "Kitchen's."

*Surprise in The Wissahickon: Thomas Mill Bridge.*

Today The Wissahickon—as the area is affectionately known—comprises a 1000-acre tract attached to Fairmount Park. And, unknown to most Philadelphians, Thomas Mill covered bridge still perches over the stream. With the busy city all about, it can be reached only by foot or on horseback either by way of the level path from Bell's Mills Bridge above, or by dropping down the old steep road from Chestnut Hill to the northeast. The hike is well worth the effort, for the old bridge with its saw-tooth portals is in a cool and inviting tract of wooded park and picnic area.

## THE SUSQUEHANNA WATERSHED

The Susquehanna, Pennsylvania's greatest river, drains the vast central region of the state. There were once over thirty covered bridges across this river and its main branches; big important ones which helped to give life and growth to the highways that crossed them and the little towns they served. This was, and is, ideal covered bridge country, with timber-clad hills and adequate stone for abutments.

The Susquehanna's first tentative dip into Pennsylvania took it flowing under twin railroad bridges at Susquehanna, and a long highway structure at Great Bend. After another sojourn through New York State the river enters Keystone territory for good, and once passed below covered spans at Athens and Towanda; the latter, built by one John Bottom, was known for decades as The Old Wagon Bridge.

*Rickrack trim titivated this old crossing over Wissahickhon Creek.*

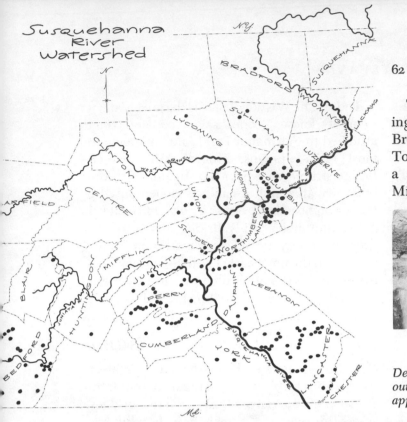

Susquehanna
River
Watershed

Today Bradford County has but one surviving example—a well-designed arch span over Brown's Creek near Luther's Mills west of Towanda. All Luzerne County can boast of is a private covered bridge near Huntington Mills.

*Knapp Bridge near Luther's Mills.*

*Death of a bridge: North Branch ice in 1904 takes out Danville's pride as townsfolk watch, first crack appears (arrow), last span awaits fate.*

*Columbia spans are, l. to r., Knoebel's Grove, one of Catawissa's, and one of three near Pensyl's Mill.*

The picture changes in Columbia, Pennsylvania's tied-for-first covered bridge county. With streams entering the North Branch from both north and south, this hilly, wooded region has timber crossings in every direction, and a covered bridge fancier can seek out nearly forty of them within easy driving distance of Bloomsburg. They range from the 185-footer at Rupert to little weatherbeaten spans on the remote upper reaches of Little Fishing and Roaring Creeks.

John H. Edson of New Columbus was a top builder in this area. He replaced the great flood-wrecked Susquehanna bridges at Berwick and Catawissa. Most of the remaining older arch bridges in Columbia County bear evidence attesting to Edson's careful work: true squared arches, flat, gracefully rounded portals and trim siding. His Fishing Creek Bridge in the Boro of Stillwater, built in 1849, was re-dedicated a hundred and two years later as "a lasting historical memorial to all Columbia County bridges." This was an unusual step to take for a county so rich in examples, and such pride in old landmarks could well be emulated elsewhere.

Stillwater Bridge is now used only for pedestrian traffic. Nearby are the Twin Bridges just east of Forks which form a unique crossing consisting of two separate spans of different ages and types of construction, built within a few feet of each other over the divided channels of Huntington Creek. Walter Pennington of Danville held his first job during the construction of the southernmost of the Twins. He was a very conscientious water boy—aged six!

Knoebel's Grove, a large and well-patronized amusement park, is located on Columbia's Northumberland County line. Within three miles of this spot, in both counties, are six regular covered highway bridges. In the park itself is an authentic span which originally stood at Benton, some fifty miles to the north; in 1937 it was moved and re-erected here. In addition, Knoebel's Grove also has a nice little pedestrian crossing, quite probably the only inter-county covered footbridge in the United States. Serving the park's miniature railroad is a two-span covered structure over Mugser Run, which doubles, boarded up, as a carbarn for the train in winter. Visitors to Knoebel's Grove can't help but go away covered-bridge conscious.

Far to the west another arm of the Susquehanna starts its long journey to the sea. At McGee's Mills in Clearfield County is the only covered bridge which actually still spans the great river or its main branches. Others—the long one at Clearfield; Lock Haven with its towpath and pretentious brick tollhouse, and bridges at Williamsport and Muncy—succumbed to fire, ice jams and the tremendous springtime floods. At Lewisburg the covered bridge carried both highway traffic and the

*Pedestrians paid at the fancy tollhouse, shared Lock Haven's sidewalk with canalers' mules.*

*Only McGee's Mills, carried over West Branch by its 107-foot Burr arch, remains on the Susquehanna.*

little Lewisburg & Tyrone Railroad until 1906. Blue Hill Bridge, at Northumberland, was the West Branch's longest-lived: ninety-five years

old when it was destroyed in a fire of suspicious origin in 1923.

Only a handful of covered bridges dot the

*Item for bridge and/or car fans: late model poses in 1924 with former Muncy span near Mawrglen.*

*Main Susquehanna River starts at Northumberland, where Burr's North Branch (half shows upper center) and Field's West Branch crossing stood when this shot was taken.*

valley of the West Branch now. There are little spans over back-country creeks near Tylersville, Buttonwood, Cogan House and Lairdsville. The Loyalsock Creek, which once had a roofed span at nearly every crossing, still has two big ones on its upper course in Sullivan County. The one serving the village of Forksville, well over a century old, nearly went out in an ice jam during the Winter of 1958–59.

Back of Lewisburg in Union County is a semi-abandoned bridge few people care to cross, for it leads into the grounds of the Federal Penitentiary. Millmont has a refurbished red and white span over Penn Creek with a stern admonition *not* to remove any boards for high and dry fishing.

Big John Dunkelberger had an adventure with the bridge on Fourth Street right at the edge of Mifflinburg Boro. Bringing a large load of hay into town, the wagon lurched and he was brushed off as the team entered the bridge. While John clung desperately, the departing hayrack caught the cuff of his pants and set up a terrific strain on his galluses. The horses trotted dutifully on, the load trailed wisps of hay, lanky John clutched for a handhold on the bridge portal, his suspenders stretched out as though about to launch him— and man and trousers parted company.

Hollering bloody murder, Dunkelberger hung there by his fingertips until a neighbor lady fetched a ladder. By this time the team was out of sight around the corner in town. The bemused lady, who had originally come from the "Dutch country," was nearly as flustered as the red-faced man.

"My stars, John," she reproved him mildly, "climbing on bridges, without britches you shouldn't!"

Another major tributary of the Susquehanna is the fabled "Blue Juniata." This stream's main branches rise in Bedford and Somerset Counties to flow generally northward. Successive mountain ranges, like a crumpled bedspread, bar its path, but the Juniata cuts through them in wild narrows to empty into the Susquehanna

near Duncannon. The Juniata was the path of empire, the canal and later railroad travel route from Philadelphia to Pittsburgh; with towns like Mifflin, Port Royal, Mexico and Millerstown sprouting up on both its banks to be served by covered bridges.

Over the Juniata's Raystown Branch, which winds and twists through Bedford County, stood one of the state's best-remembered covered bridges: Juniata Crossings on old Pennsylvania State Route 1 just west of Breezewood. The highway was a main artery carrying traffic across the state, and a big stone tavern greeted many a dusty traveler as he emerged from the bridge. Built in 1818, two-span, 367-foot Juniata Crossings originally was a double-barrel. Sometime during the last century one span of the bridge was replaced with a wide arch-truss of only one roadway. The new arrangement served well enough until automobiles began to become more numerous; then the speeding motorist, ducking into what was apparently a single-lane bridge, was suddenly confronted with a center truss looming up in the gloom dead ahead. The lost rubber from tires brought to a screeching halt practically paved the floor. Still, Juniata Crossings survived even after it was by-passed by present U.S. 30, and was a hundred and eighteen years old when it departed on the crest of the great ice flood of March, 1936.

*Juniata's murderous truss began at mid-bridge.*

*Bedford County arch near Ryot.*

*Wagner's Bridge in Perry County.*

Even at sixty miles an hour, those who go barreling along the Pennsylvania Turnpike cannot help but notice the covered bridge over the Raystown Branch near Mann's Choice. This was built in 1902 by Wilson H. Williams, and is a twentieth-century example of Burr's old arch-truss. Most of Bedford County's covered bridges date from 1870 to 1900, and a good number of them were built by Williams, a carpenter-contractor from nearby Akersville in Fulton County. West of Mann's Choice two more covered bridges can be seen from the Pennsy Pike, but it is best not to let the car's driver join in peering for a hasty glimpse of them!

Blair County has one covered bridge still standing near Tyrone, and a single well-preserved specimen is located near Shade Gap in Huntingdon County. There are four in Juniata County including sturdy spans near McCoysville and at Academia. Perry County has four times as many, some of them old arch bridges that have been reinforced externally and internally by the addition of auxiliary queenpost trusses and center piers. Although Perry was rich in hemlock woodlots, it was cheaper in the days just after the Civil War to buy sizable precut timber from the raftsmen who, to the tune of a rowdy song, floated it down the Susquehanna.

Loads of hop poles, corn and potatoes ac-

counted for a good deal of the Winter traffic over the Waggoner's Gap road south from Perry County. Often the local boys would draw in sledloads of snow to cover the floors of the main road bridges, and thus offer a smooth passage for the runners of heavily laden sleighs. Grinning and hoping for the "toll" of a penny for their efforts, the boys would stand by. All too often their only pay was an attempted whiplash; but there was sweet revenge in pelting the offending driver with hard-packed snowballs.

The old Clark's Ferry bridge used to stretch for nearly a mile across the wide Susquehanna near its junction with the Juniata. This was the last of the giant bridges of the lower river to go; it was not replaced until 1925. At Harrisburg were Theodore Burr's tandem bridges which arched up and over the Susquehanna. Charles Dickens, on his American tour in 1841, described them thus:

"We crossed the river by a wooden bridge, roofed and covered on all sides, and nearly a mile in length. It was profoundly dark, perplexed with great beams crossing and re-crossing . . . and through the chinks and crevices in the floor, the rapid river gleamed far down below like a legion of eyes."

The English author tells of the horses stumbling and floundering in the unlighted bridge, and how the confinement of the dark passage

*Mile-long Clark's Ferry Bridge in Dauphin County stood longest over the lower Susquehanna.*

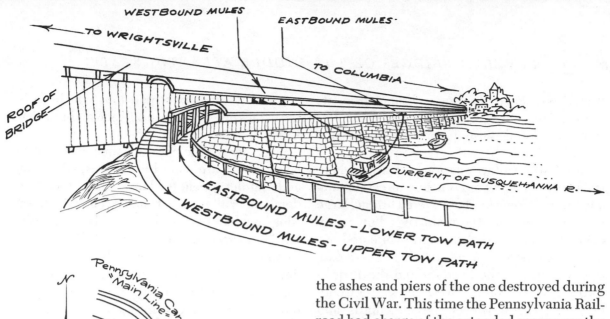

ROOF OF BRIDGE

TO WRIGHTSVILLE

WESTBOUND MULES

EASTBOUND MULES·

TO COLUMBIA

CURRENT OF SUSQUEHANNA R. →

EASTBOUND MULES - LOWER TOW PATH

WESTBOUND MULES - UPPER TOW PATH

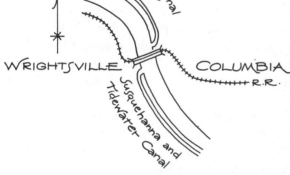

N

Pennsylvania Canal "Main Line"

WRIGHTSVILLE    COLUMBIA R.R.

Susquehanna and Tidewater Canal

made him feel as though the rafters overhead were pressing in on him.

The easterly section of the Harrisburg crossing washed out in the freshet of 1846. Replaced, it burned twenty years later; a third covered bridge on the site, with a level floor, stood until smashed by flood in 1902. The ungainly original bridge over the western channel outlasted the three versions of its twin. It had "swoops" in its arched roadway that were the delight of latter-day cyclists. (See illustration on page 12.) Harrisburgers affectionately dubbed it Old Camelback Bridge, and lamented its passing in 1903.

Down at Columbia-Wrightsville, a third "longest covered bridge in the world" arose on the ashes and piers of the one destroyed during the Civil War. This time the Pennsylvania Railroad had charge of the extended spans over the Susquehanna. They built a wide roadway between Howe trusses, with an iron section in the middle of the structure to serve as a firebreak. Both the railroad and vehicles used the bridge, and there was an auxiliary ferry alongside. This was for less hardy Columbians who didn't exactly relish the mile walk in the dark bridge, with the possibility of having to dodge spirited horses of both the four-footed and iron variety.

It will be recalled that the first crossing here was wrecked by ice and the second one burned by Union troops in retreat. The railroad's firebreak was no protection against the fate that befell the third one. On September 30, 1896, a tornado "with a noise like a hundred freight

*Third version of "longest covered bridge" built by the Pennsy; above, after 1896 tornado finished it.*

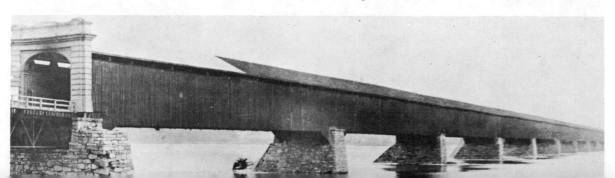

trains" wrenched the entire bridge from its piers and in a few seconds left it a mass of splintered wood and twisted iron rods in the Susquehanna.

The lower valley was long an area where travel of only a few miles in any direction took one through some kind of covered bridge, large or small. Not only the main river but nearly every tributary had them—red, white and unpainted timbered tunnels over the Shamokin, the Wisconisco, the Swatara and the Pequea to the east; and on the west across the Conodoguinet, Yellow Breeches, the Codorus, and just plain Muddy Creek. To add to the confusion there was a duplication of names. A builder who said he was erecting a bridge "over Buffalo Creek" might mean either Perry or Union County. And entirely different "Conewago" and "Mahantango" Creeks emptied into the long crooked Susquehanna River from both east and west.

Over the Wisconisco in upper Dauphin County are bridges that show a decided preference for fancy portals with such embellishments as scrolled corbels and little decorative blocks stuck to their faces. At night the silhouette of a broken entrance in the headlights of an approaching car gives the traveler the impression that he's about to be swallowed by some gap-toothed monster. Back of Harrisburg in the same county the Swatara is still

crossed by three two-span jobs which go by the names of Clifton, Sand Beach and Fiddler's Elbow.

Over across the Susquehanna in Cumberland County are more big bridges, whose age and usefulness befit the landscape of the Conodoguinet Valley. That name (in which the "dog" is silent) comes from the Indian, meaning "forever, nothing but bends." Bend the Conodoguinet does, from above Newburg down the center of Cumberland, one tortuous curve after another, until the stream empties into the mother river opposite Harrisburg. Out of thirty crossings of this creek, all but two were once covered spans. Eckert's Bridge, west of Newville, was a triplet crossing over three converging arms of the creek, and at Quigley's not far upstream were twin bridges built end to end. Today you can still visit twelve Conodoguinet survivors easily in one afternoon of exploring by car, starting from Ramp's, east of Newburg, and going down to Sporting Hill, where stands asphalt-paved Erb's Bridge, the second longest covered bridge in Pennsylvania.

In the 1860's, the newly patented Moseley Tubular Iron Arch Bridge was adopted by Cumberland County Commissioners, and ten on this design were erected in the area. Not one survives today, and Burgner's and Silver Spring covered spans across the Conodoguinet replaced two of them in the 1880's. Although the original Moseley arch crossing has been gone for three quarters of a century, the Silver Spring wooden structure is still often referred to locally as Old Iron Bridge.

Of special note in Cumberland is Hays Bridge, out of sight of the Pennsylvania Turn-

*Fancy rest for Fiddler's Elbow.*

*America's oldest: Hay's Bridge.*

*Some Representative Portals from the Author's Sketchbook.*

pike behind a ridge west of Carlisle. This conventional Burr arch-truss bridge is 110 feet long and was built in 1825 by John and Joseph Hays for only $1,500. The pedestrian crossing over it to nearby Meadow Brook Park gets a rather eerie feeling from walking on its modern open steel grating floor, something like traversing a box with a sieve bottom. But Hays Bridge's first claim to fame lies in its having an authenticated date of erection which makes it not only the oldest existing covered bridge in Pennsylvania, but in the entire United States. During the flood of 1889 Hays Bridge stood staunch while the Conodoguinet boiled and eddied around both ends. There is a report that a man and "a woman whom he stated was his wife" were stranded for two days on the flood-washed span. Marital status aside, the couple must have undergone a harrowing experience.

Cumberland County shares two covered bridges over Yellow Breeches Creek—Spangler's and Bowmansdale—with York County to the south. Because of a replacement program in the past decade, all the county-owned covered bridges in York have been eliminated, leaving only two dilapidated structures, owned by the state, at Roler and at Bentzell's Mill, and these are slated to go. "John Finley of York County" has his name on the records as the builder of widely scattered covered bridges.

*Yellow suicide bridge at Westmont Station.*

In addition to some in his home area, Finley built average-sized Burr arches in adjacent Adams County, at least one lengthy span near Newville in Cumberland; and down in Maryland he put up two tiny ones near Blue Ball—probably only a few weeks' work for an established builder with knowledgeable carpenters.

Lebanon County lost its last covered bridge in 1949 when the old Bunker Hill crossing south of Jonestown went up in flames. An unusual bridge to the north of Lebanon suffered a similar fate more than a decade before. It was a covered overpass, spanning a curved rock cutting of the Lebanon & Tremont (Reading) Railroad at Westmont Station. With ornate portals, and painted an outlandish yellow, this

*More hard luck for Lebanon bridges: Mount Zion's rickety roadway dumps an old iron-tired tractor.*

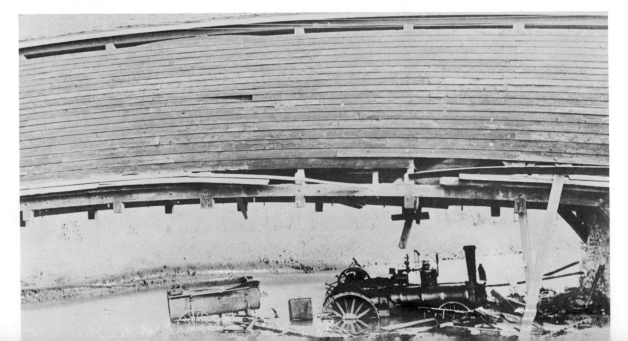

was one of a very few covered bridges in America built only to span railroad tracks. From the timbers below this bridge a despondent man once hanged himself. Unnoticed by passers-by above, the dangling body was first picked out by a horrified engineer as it was caught in the glare of his locomotive's headlight.

Lancaster, with nearly forty roofed spans, ties Columbia as Pennsylvania's "covered bridge county." In general, the bridges are trim and well kept, entirely adequate to serve the lightly traveled arteries on which they are situated. The typical stone Pennsylvania parapets are very much in evidence in Lancaster, as are such touches as interior whitewash, board-and-batten finish, and several coats of red or white paint.

A lot of care went into building covered bridges in Lancaster, and that care accounts for the fact that at least a third of all the roofed bridges ever built in the county are still standing. As was the practice elsewhere in Pennsylvania, the county commissioners contracted for the building of bridges and laid down detailed and minute specifications as to just how they were to be constructed. When a bridge was finished, the county court would appoint competent inspectors to see that it had been erected according to the contract.

The Lancaster inspectors believed in carrying out their jobs to the letter. When they were called in to examine Weaver's (or Shearer's) Mill Bridge, built in 1878 north of Goodville, these gimlet-eyed gentlemen went to work on the structure with their tape lines. They clambered all over the bridge and then declared that the clear roadway was only thirteen feet wide instead of the specified fourteen. That was enough to knock a deduction off the builder's pay. Also, the inspecting team went on to declare, the eaves were two inches short. And a piece of the floor joisting contained "very imperfect wood." Despite their skimpiness the eaves of Shearer's Mill Bridge have now been keeping the wet off the timbers for well over eighty years. Perhaps if the final inspection of

*Shearer's Bridge south of Lancaster Junction.*

*Fine Burr span on Conestoga Creek near Hinkeltown.*

*Shenk's Mill Bridge near Salunga.*

*Snavely's Mill is state's longest covered bridge.*

other covered bridges in the state had been as tough as this one, there might be an additional half a hundred left standing in a good many other counties.

Covered bridges serve Lancaster County's well-known Amish sect, too. Since rubber tires are banned by their Church, the Amish use tractors whose wheels are treaded with steel cleats and they get around in closed iron-tired buggies. To prevent wear and tear on the wooden bridge floors, steel plates are laid as runners through those near the homes of the "plain people."

The best way to see Lancaster's covered bridges is to take a leisurely two days, following one creek at a time. The Big and Little Chickies Creek watershed east of Marietta has a "nest" of eight, and the valley of the Pequea Creek south of Lancaster proudly retains a similar number. Still another eight span Big Conestoga Creek on its meanderings from Churchtown to Safe Harbor. The longest of these is Snavely's Mill, or Second Lock, Bridge just southwest of the city of Lancaster. Two spans over the Conestoga give this century-old landmark a length of 349 feet, making it the longest covered bridge in all of Pennsylvania.

Adams County's Conewago Creek bridges must be included with those of the Susquehanna. Once red, in recent years they have been painted gray and white, with black and white warning stripes on the portals. Four such bridges are near Irishtown south of U.S. 30.

## THE POTOMAC WATERSHED

The Potomac basin, which drains the southern portion of the central counties bordering on Maryland, was never blessed with many covered bridges. Like the land beyond the Mason-Dixon Line it was quarry country; and stone was the predominant building material. Exceptions are two covered bridges west of Greencastle in Franklin County, plus two in Adams County south of Gettysburg.

Best known of the latter is Sauk's Bridge southwest of Gettysburg. Built in 1854, it served both Armies during the great battle which raged nearby, and survived: miraculously some general did not decide to burn it. Now it spans a quiet pool of Marsh Creek only

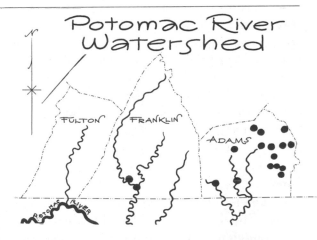

a short way from the farm and occasional country White House of Dwight D. Eisenhower.

*Neighbors and history make Sauk's Bridge famous.*

## THE ERIE WATERSHED

In the extreme northwestern portion of Pennsylvania, five covered bridges serve Erie County on country roads back in from the lake. East of Waterford is a span whose builder favored Mr. Town's lattice type of construction. Crossing Elk Creek under a sightly bluff is the little "Gudgeonville" bridge near Girard, and in addition there are still three small bridges west of Albion. One of these, over Conneaut

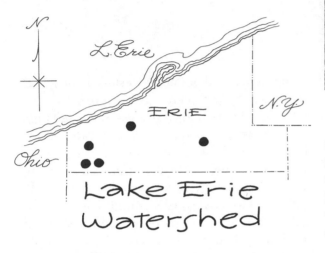

*Picturesque Gudgeonville Bridge.*

Creek near Cherry Hill, has a portal on which is painted STINES & WINGATE—CLOTHING. County crews occasionally renew the large old lettering with fresh paint, even though the advertiser, a firm in Conneaut, Ohio, has been out of business for fifty years!

## THE OHIO WATERSHED

As most casual map-readers are aware, the Allegheny River meets the Monongahela at the apex of Pittsburgh's Golden Triangle to become the mighty Ohio. To streamline our procedure in locating Pennsylvania's covered bridges according to the five watersheds, the Pennsylvania portion of the Ohio River and all the land drained by the Allegheny, the Monongahela, and their major and minor tributaries, is considered as the Ohio Valley watershed.

Water which ultimately runs into the Ohio flows under practically all the state's covered bridges west of the Alleghenies. The lumber and oil boom counties to the north went directly from primitive strapped log crossings to iron spans, and for the most part skipped the intermediate age of covered bridges. There were exceptions, of course, like the very early

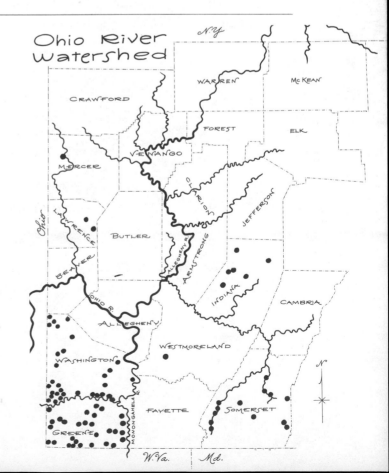

*Rare Cochranton Bridge used lots of lumber.*

Long truss bridge built over Brokenstraw Creek at Irvine; the lengthy Cochranton Bridge, and the Oil Creek railroad crossing—with Oil City advertising by Oil City merchants on its sides. Clarion had a big bridge which James Moore traveled many miles to build. Emlenton and Foxburg had crossings of the Allegheny, and for many years the double-barreled Black Bridge did service, surrounded by Carnegie's steel mills, in the heart of New Castle.

Only a handful dot northwestern Pennsylvania today. Near Greenville in Mercer County is the Kidd's Mill Bridge over the Shenango River. This span is built with the little-known Smith Patent Truss, a geometrical arrangement of timbers which is stronger than it appears to be. It was patented in 1867 by Robert W. Smith of Tippecanoe City, Ohio. The inventor formed his own company to build bridges of his design. The firm was active in the Middle and Far West, but today Kidd's Mill is the only one of Smith's patent bridges standing east of Ohio.

Five Town lattice spans still standing in Indiana County make an island of this "mode" in a sea of Burr arches. Westmoreland County's sole survivor is a fine century-old structure with horizontal siding over Big Sewickley Creek at Bell's Mill, east of West Union.

*One of two neat Town spans near Davis.*

*Kidd's Mill (top) and Smith truss plan.*

Lawrence County had a covered bridge that lived up to its advance billing. Located over the deep gorge of Jones Run was the old Breakneck Bridge—it passed from the scene when a coal truck crashed into and through it, killing the driver. North of its site in the Slippery Rock Valley is McConnell's Mills Bridge, one of but four Howe truss highway bridges in Pennsylvania. Here the bridge and its adjacent recreation areas are part of a new state park.

It has been many years since Pittsburgh, the metropolis of western Pennsylvania, had a covered bridge of its own. At various times, though, at least ten roofed wooden crossings served the smoky city at the head of the Ohio.

The first to be built was the one planned by Lewis Wernwag and constructed by Joseph Thompson over the Monongahela at Smithfield Street. This long, multiple-arch toll bridge was a financial success from the day it was completed in 1818. Its outstanding feature was the toll collector's living quarters. He was housed in a small apartment built above the barnlike portal on the Pittsburgh side.

The following year, 1819, the same builders erected Pittsburgh's first Allegheny River crossing, the bridge at 6th Street. The proprietors felt so sure of having a money-maker on

*Holocaust in 1845 took Pittsburgh's first covered bridge, designed by Wernwag.*

*Lawrence County still has McConnell's Mills span.*

and nearly forgotten covered bridge had been so damaged by ice that it was replaced. This was the short-lived covered wooden canal aqueduct at 11th Street, built in 1836 across the Allegheny for the Pennsylvania Canal. This unique structure was, in effect, a giant trough carried 1,134 feet over the river on close-set piers. Mules clopped along on the raised towpath inside the bridge, hauling heavy cargo boats across to Allegheny City. Charles Dickens described this crossing too, in his *American Notes:* "Another dreamy place . . . stranger than the bridge at Harrisburg . . . a vast low wooden chamber full of water."

It is estimated that the water enclosed in the canal trunk across the seven spans weighed nearly two thousand tons. This enormous weight was no insurance against the external force of the Allegheny's ice packs. This strangest of roofed crossings was hopelessly damaged after standing for only half a dozen years and was replaced in 1844–45. The great John A. Roebling, who climaxed his engineering career by planning Brooklyn Bridge, built his very first suspension bridge, a new aqueduct, on the 11th Street site. The designer used timbers of the old aqueduct for scaffolding and melted down a great quantity of its good iron bolts to make his new wire cables.

their hands that they celebrated the bridge's opening with a huge banquet. They had tables laid from end to end of the new floorboards, and toasted, wined and dined visiting dignitaries in fine style. Waiters formed a long procession from a nearby hotel and suffered from fallen arches before everybody was served. This novel dining hall was used for public transportation for forty years. Its contemporary across town at Smithfield Street caught fire on an April afternoon in 1845. The tollkeeper lost his cozy home atop the bridge, and nearly forty acres of Pittsburgh went up in flames along with it.

Even before that, though, a most unusual

Union Bridge at the Point spanned the Allegheny from 1874 to 1912. It was a long Howe truss with ornate stone portals, auxiliary arches and twin sidewalks. The 43rd Street Bridge was the last to go; it was torn down in 1924.

A favorite crossing for Pittsburghers was the

*Union Bridge's Howe truss over the Allegheny competed with Monongahela suspension span at right.*

Hand, or 9th, Street Bridge, built in 1839. It had a boardwalk the length of its roof, intended as a promenade for fashionable ladies and gentlemen. However, it proved to be too windy for pleasant strolling. When it became a hangout for unsavory characters the authorities had to close it off.

Hand Street Bridge was the scene of one of Pittsburgh's early-day practical jokes. During the summer of 1846 it was advertised extensively that on a certain day a Frenchman, M. Anser, would fly from the top of the bridge. Gawpers thronged the riverbanks at the appointed time. Finally a man in a long black cloak appeared on the promenade and strode to the center of the long bridge. Poised dramatically, he threw back his cape and produced a large gray goose which he tossed into the air. As the bird flapped away, those who knew their French felt chagrined they hadn't guessed—but hastily explained to their friends that Mr. Goose had, indeed, flown as promised.

When it came time to replace the 9th Street Bridge in 1890, a Chicago match company contracted to buy the old white pine timbers which made up its trusses. The demolition firm found the arches so well-built that it was impossible to topple them over into the Allegheny: they had to be cut away panel by panel. The match people were disappointed, too. Over the fifty-one years that the bridge had stood, the originally easy-to-work white pine had hardened and become tough as gum. Axes wielded against it simply bounced. The old 9th Street Bridge went to make pilings and cofferdams—but not matchsticks.

Covered bridges were among the victims of the great Johnstown Flood of 1889. When the wall of water came plunging down from the broken South Fork Dam to engulf the city, the maddened Conemaugh smashed to kingdom come both the two-span covered structure at Johnstown and the big Blairsville Bridge beyond. Nobody ever found any identifiable pieces. The force of the water had slowed by the time it reached Saltsburg farther down-

*Long Barronvale Bridge in Somerset County.*

stream, and the timbered tunnel over the Kiskiminetas withstood the onslaught.

Somerset is a mountain-top county with more than a dozen covered bridges. They are kept painted an attractive bright barn red with white trim. Somerset's bridges span streams which drain off in four directions to feed the Susquehanna, the Potomac, the Allegheny and the Monongahela. Near New Lexington are a fine "run" of old red bridges over Laurel Hill Creek—at Barronvale, Kings, and Upper and Lower Humbert.

Earl W. Dickey of Altoona tells the story of a hair-raising encounter his great-uncle, Dr. Harmer D. Moore of New Lexington, had on a covered bridge during his rounds in the Laurel Hill Mountains toward the close of the last century.

One steaming summer night "Doc" Moore made a late call on horseback. It was well past midnight when he finally started down the mountainside toward the covered bridge over Laurel Hill Creek. The night was overcast but the moon shone occasionally through rifts in the clouds. At the western end of the bridge the horse snorted and stopped short. With much urging, he forced her nearer the bridge. Then he heard footsteps. The good doctor's scalp prickled when a stray shaft of moonlight revealed a tall figure in white running out of the bridge shadows and off up the country road.

Medical men don't believe in ghosts, but "Doc" allowed he was mighty nervous. The apparition climbed a fence and seemed to flit from bush to tree trunk, causing his badly spooked horse to plunge with fright. Thoroughly alarmed now, Moore rode up to the next farmhouse and banged mightily on the door. The men he roused returned with him to make a thorough search for the ghost. What they finally caught in the woods was the farmer's own bean pole of a wife, red-faced even in the moonlight. Bothered by the heat and sleeplessness, she'd got in the habit of taking a midnight walk in her flimsy nightdress to cool off in the bridge. "Doc" Moore always considered his meeting with the "ghost" of Laurel Hill Creek covered bridge his most unnerving experience.

Rural southwestern Pennsylvania once fairly teemed with covered bridges. In Greene and Washington Counties there were at least two hundred of them only fifty years ago, with other estimates from reputable authorities reaching as high as four hundred! They were scattered over both large and small streams

*Wartime prompted tidy Lippincott Bridge.*

from Aunt Clara's Fork of King's Creek, through Tenmile Creek and its much longer branch valleys, down to little Coon Run in the extreme southwest corner of the state. Construction for the most part involved king- and queenpost trusses of the kind that any competent carpenter from Bentleyville to Bobtown was fully capable of erecting. Northwest of Mather is a little kingpost covered bridge put up in 1943 when the wartime shortage of steel made wooden timbers a most practical bridge building material once again. It is the youngest such structure on a public highway in Pennsylvania.

Perhaps typical of the entire region was the Ackley Bridge, built over Enslow's Fork of Wheeling Creek. Located on the county line, both Greene and Washington financed the

*Gabby Bridge skeleton, jacked up by wooden pier, sagged on Chartiers Creek in Washington County.*

erecting of the bridge in 1832, but it fell to the folks in the neighborhood to put it up. Joshua Ackley and Daniel Clouse were the principal builders.

For a hundred and five years the 75-foot span served faithfully. Then it was presented to Henry Ford, who for a decade had been in the market for a covered bridge to add to his old-time village at Dearborn, Michigan. His agents had examined bridges that were about to be replaced in several states, but they were all either too long and large for convenient dismantling, or the misguided authorities set some exorbitant price on title to them. When this little intercounty Pennsylvania span was to be razed, it was acquired from the state by Joshua Ackley's granddaughter, who in turn *gave* it to Mr. Ford.

As soon as the Fork had frozen in November, 1937, Ford's workmen lowered the bridge onto the ice and carefully dismantled it. A sudden thaw made it nip-and-tuck work. The last timber had scarcely been stowed aboard a truck before the ice broke up and moved off downstream.

Ackley Bridge holds the American long-distance record for moving a covered bridge. Nearly three hundred miles away in Dearborn, it is now perfectly restored and spans an artificial river especially dug to go under it. Just as it was a century ago, Pennsylvania's famous "exported bridge" is crossed only by horse-drawn carriages which transport thousands of visitors through Ford's famous Greenfield Village. It makes a fine monument to covered bridges everywhere.

*Ackley Bridge at its original site, above; shined up for Ford's Greenfield Village.*

# VIRGINIA: Serving the Old Dominion

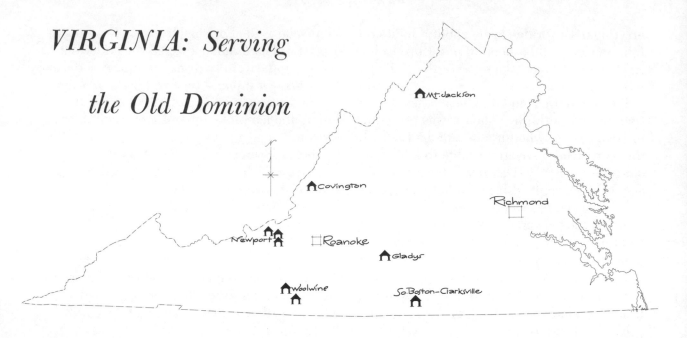

DESPITE THE TOLL of the War between the States, and the terrible floods of 1870 and 1878, there are records of nearly a hundred covered bridges that once carried Virginia's highways. Only nine still stand today. Tidewater Virginia, the whole eastern section of the Commonwealth, just never did have any covered bridges. South Side Virginia had a few, as did the western tip of the state. But for the most part, the popularity of roofed spans for crossing rivers was centered in that beautiful strip of land beyond the vast hump of the Blue Ridge—the Valley of Virginia. Here the mountains had the oak and softwoods for beams and chords and The Valley provided the bridge sites.

The original flow of pioneer travel followed Virginia's rivers, rather than crossed them. In time, turnpikes were punched through the passes and over the ridge gaps to open up the western counties and carry settlers and commerce toward the promised land of Ohio. As was the case elsewhere in America, Virginian toll roads needed substantial covered wooden bridges, and spots at which they crossed often became the sites of sizable towns.

Generally speaking, each of the several regions specialized in one particular covered bridge plan. The South Side counties, for instance, favored the Town lattice type of construction. This popularity is explained by the fact that the inventor, Ithiel Town, first built and promoted his distinctive crisscross spans in neighboring North Carolina. Carpenters who examined a Town lattice bridge down Fayetteville or Salisbury way went home to build similar structures—after making sure that the canny transplanted Yankee had been paid his $1-per-foot royalty. The Appalachian foothills from Maryland to Alabama were dotted with this type of bridge. A Virginia carpenter and contractor who specialized in this design was Granville Montgomery of Floyd. In addition to his home area, he operated in Carroll, Patrick and Henry Counties. When it was replaced in 1944, Montgomery's Little River Bridge north of Floyd was the last of the Town lattice spans in the Old Dominion.

*Lynchburg's old James River crossing.*

Another "pocket" of a particular bridge type centered around South Boston along the southern border of the state. Here the favored plan was the Haupt truss, invented in 1839 by Gettysburg's engineering genius, Herman Haupt, whom we have already met in battle-dress during the War. His truss was a system of combining paired lattice timbers with king-posts. It was never extensively popular although, through the medium of his *General Theory of Bridge Construction,* local carpenters in widely separated areas picked up Haupt's bridge building ideas. The book was published in 1851 and became a standard text during the next twenty-five years. And plenty of copies were still around after that.

Certainly one of them must have been well-thumbed in Halifax County. In this area nearly a dozen of the old-time Haupt covered bridges were erected during the present century. All but one are gone now. The survivor was built in 1908 to cross Hyco River just north of U.S. 58 between South Boston and Clarksville. It is one of three Haupt truss covered bridges in America. The others are in North Carolina and Vermont.

Also put up in the 1900's—but using diminutive Burr arches—are the three little Sinking Creek bridges near Newport in Giles County. Of the two over Smith River near Woolwine in Patrick County, one dates from 1920, thus making it Virginia's youngest covered bridge. It presents a novel appearance from having the openwork between its queenpost truss members packed with boarding, and a traveler feels as if he was crossing between solid wooden walls.

The by-passed Marysville Bridge (over Seneca River southeast of Gladys) in Campbell County is still standing. It is reached by long, open trestlework and has unusual zebra

*At the right are five of Virginia's nine existing covered bridges; starting at top is the Haupt South Boston-Clarksville crossing of Hyco River; then, the private Maple Shade Bridge, the unused span near Newport, and a big red bridge—all Burr arches over Sinking Creek and all in Giles County; and, last, the elder Woolwine bridge on Smith River.*

*Marysville warning, left, and Woolwine's baby.*

striping painted on the portals as a safety measure to outline the clearance of the bridge.

Far to the north in The Valley's apple country stands the longest covered bridge remaining in Virginia, the last of such crossings of the Shenandoah River and its tributaries. Meems Bottom Bridge, just south of Mount Jackson, is carried by a faultlessly constructed wooden arch in the grand tradition of Theodore Burr and stretches 191 feet in a single span over the North Fork of the Shenandoah. Meems Bottom was erected in 1892–93 under the supervision of F. H. Wisler. Mr. Wisler built well, with particular attention to draining off rain and surface water which might otherwise stay to rot the bridge. It is noteworthy, too, for its heavy masonry block abutments and matched horizontal siding.

Just by chance, two covered bridges that once stood in the Old Dominion have been given national renown. A composite picture

*Meems Bottom Bridge in best Burr style.*

of them appeared in 1952 on the postage stamp issued to commemorate the hundredth anniversary of the American Society of Civil Engineers.

The society's centenary committee thought that the contrast between a bridge of 1852 and one typical of 1952 would be appropriate. The George Washington Suspension Bridge at New York was a natural for the modern structure, but selecting an old-time specimen proved a bit more difficult: the committee sent "about two hundred" photographs of covered bridges to the Post Office Department's artists in Washington to choose from.

When the design was made, and even before the stamp was issued, a "source picture" of the bridge selected was released to the newspapers, together with the information that the engraving showed the former Spruce Grove Bridge spanning the West Branch of Octoraro Creek in Lancaster County, Pennsylvania. This was an error, unfortunately repeated in good faith by both the engineering and philatelic press. In reality the main photograph used in designing the stamp was one of the Buffalo Forge Bridge, which used to cross Buffalo Creek near Buena Vista, Virginia. It had been built in 1878, given a roof in 1882, and was abandoned and razed in 1946.

This wasn't all. To present wider proportions and more portal details for the bridge on the ASCE stamp, designer Victor S. McCloskey, Jr., used a second photograph—also of a former Virginia covered bridge. His embellishments were copied from an old print of the long bridge over the Rivanna River at Palmyra. This bridge had been burned purposely in 1932 after a new crossing was built some distance downstream.

However, although such detective work tickles the fancy of dyed-in-the-wool engineering historians, delving into the archives is secondary to the very real satisfaction of seeing American covered bridges honored on something so widely used as a postage stamp.

Mindful of the bleak future of covered

*Buffalo Forge, top, furnished truss and sides, Palmyra's span (center) gave portals to stamp below.*

bridges, Virginia has a good record of leaving her old spans standing as historical monuments alongside their modern replacements. But flood and fire have taken their toll, and the efforts of local citizens to keep unused covered bridges in good repair have met with scant success.

One such bridge was the old two-lane crossing of North River at Lexington. It was erected in 1877 and carried generations of Lexingtonians across the broad stream; and even, for part of its existence, extolled the virtues of WACOMA—THE PERFECT CURE in an advertisement painted along the exterior of its siding. When the old arch span was by-passed and retired in 1935, the local chapter of the Association for the Preservation of Virginia Antiquities took over its maintenance. The group had high hopes for the old landmark but preserving it proved difficult. The bridge became a gathering spot for local toughs, and was regarded by mounted cadets from neighboring Virginia Military Institute as the ideal place for cavalry charges. Boards disappeared, tin sections of roof blew off, timbers rotted. Regretfully, APVA had the bridge taken down in 1944.

Another attempt at preservation put the

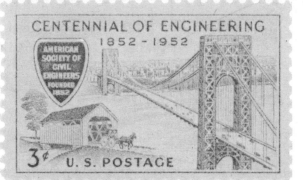

Buffalo Forge Bridge at nearby Buena Vista into the hands of an APVA affiliate in 1940. Little money was available, and the bridge was off the beaten path. During the years of World War II it received little attention, and possession finally reverted to the adjoining property owner, D. E. Brady. Mr. Brady had Buffalo Forge torn down seven years before the civil engineers' postage stamp forever memorialized it.

Alleghany County, high in the ranges of the western edge of the Commonwealth, must have been a toll-road surveyor's nightmare: in the early days the James River & Kanawha Turnpike crossed seven covered bridges in sixteen miles. Among them were big Burr arch bridges at Covington and Clifton Forge, dating from the 1830's. When the original Clifton Forge crossing washed away it was replaced in 1888 with a roofed structure on Howe's design. Today, from a total of at least ten covered spans—the most of record in any Virginia county—Alleghany has just one remaining: the famous Humpback Bridge.

It is by far the oldest covered span in the state and its singular construction is unduplicated anywhere in America. The story of Old Humpback gives a happier side of Virginia's preservation picture.

Originally there were three Humpback Bridges to the west of Covington, all built in 1835 within a mile of each other to swerve the turnpike back and forth over Dunlop Creek. Contractor for the three crossings was a Mr. Venable from Lewisburg (now West Virginia), and the facts handed down say that his principal axeman was an eighteen-year-old named Thomas Kincaid. It was Kincaid's job to fell the oaks and hew the timbers by hand. Then he shaped the locust pins which would fasten the truss members together.

To support the heavy Conestoga wagons rolling out to Kentucky and Ohio, Venable used multiple-kingpost trusses with curved upper and lower chords. And instead of hanging a level floor in the usual manner, he put his beams and planking directly on the lower line of the arch. The bridges were duly roofed and weatherboarded horizontally to conform to the curve. Naturally they were dubbed the Humpback Bridges by local folk, and their fame was made.

One of the Humpbacks was burned during the War between the States and a second succumbed to raging high water in 1913. The third, and easternmost, is still standing near Covington, retired after having carried increasing traffic for eighty-six years. It has a clear span of exactly 100 feet from abutment to abutment. The actual length of roadway is longer, though, because the rise of the arch lifts the floor 8 feet higher in the middle than it is at the ends. In 1929 a new crossing for the Midland Trail was built nearby and this last Humpback Bridge was left to a nearby farmer who occasionally stored it full of hay.

Then came the growth of wayside parks on Virginia highways, and the Covington Chamber of Commerce thought to spend $5000 to purchase five acres at the Humpback site and make the old bridge a first-rate tourist attraction. The Covington Business and Professional Women's Club volunteered to raise the money, and appointed a special committee headed by Miss Helen V. Childs to do the job. Miss Childs worked and talked up the bridge project so enthusiastically that some of her friends took to calling her "Miss Humpback." Funds were solicited from the county and the city; from eighty-eight business firms and professional men, thirty-seven civic and fraternal organizations and from over six hundred individuals—all over the country.

The $5000 raised to buy the site was matched by an equal sum from the Virginia State Highway Department. The bridge, unused for twenty-five years but still in good shape, was re-sided, painted, and rededicated with appropriate ceremonies on May 26, 1954.

Old Humpback, now nearing the century-and-a-quarter mark, has trembled to the passage of herds of cattle, huge freight wagons, and Union and Confederate armies. Many a

*Clifton Forge's replacement had crop-eared canopies.*

*The span's Howe truss detail.*

Model T bounced up and over its roadway in
the early years of motoring. Today it is quiet,
with only an occasional small footpassenger
who voices the query:

"Daddy, why did they build such a *funny*
bridge?"

# WEST VIRGINIA: *Mountain Timber Carries On*

BECAUSE WEST VIRGINIA did not attain statehood until 1863, many of its covered bridges were (and some still are) older than the Mountain State itself. They were scattered across two thirds of West Virginia's fifty-five counties and could be found on main thoroughfares and rutted back roads from the

Mason-Dixon line of the Pennsylvania border to within hailing distance of Kentucky.

Again it was the turnpikes, sanctioned by the Commonwealth of Virginia, that first found use for sizable covered bridges. As early as 1811 the James River Company's directors were planning a cross-state highroad to combine a long inland canal with a passable wagon

route over the mountains to Holderby's Landing (now Huntington) on the Ohio River.

Two important bridges were necessary if the new pike was to cross the Gauley and Greenbrier Rivers. James Moore came down from Pennsylvania to supervise their construction and bark terse orders in his hybrid German-English. He built Gauley Bridge first, flinging three double-barreled spans 480 feet across the wide mouth of the river. Even the dry report of the Virginia Road Commissioner for 1825 waxed lyrical when it described it as "exceedingly beautiful, in the midst of remarkably wild scenery—the best bridge in the state."

Moore then moved his operations eastward and graced the Greenbrier at Caldwell with an equally fine bridge. Here he used only two arches to span a river width of 422 feet. With bridges like these, the James River & Kanawha Turnpike was soon in business.

On the Gauley, disgruntled ferry operators could see nothing beautiful about the new bridge that had destroyed their livelihood. Before a year was out they hired incendiaries to burn it, and rubbed their hands in glee as the great bridge went up in flames. The arsonists were caught and given prison terms, but this did not prevent two more bridges on the same abutments from meeting the same fate. War brought a legitimate boon to the ferrymen, though: the last covered Gauley Bridge on the site was put to the torch in 1861 to cover the retreat of Confederate troops.

Greenbrier Bridge was destroyed in similar fashion two years later, but its replacement in kind served the Midland Trail, the old pike's successor, until 1932.

Even better known as a great route to the West was the National Road. Leaving Cumberland, Maryland, this highway cut across the southwest corner of Pennsylvania and the narrow northern panhandle of Virginia. At

*Maybe Wernwag planned the Ohio's Belmont Bridge.*

Wheeling it reached the barrier of the Ohio River. There its travelers crossed the river's wide East Channel by ferry until 1849, when the Wheeling Suspension Bridge was first erected. The West Channel of the Ohio was crossed by the covered Belmont Bridge from Wheeling Island to Bridgeport. Built in 1836, Belmont was one of the best bridges on the Road, with double driveways and double sidewalks to accommodate the heavy traffic. This interstate crossing was the only covered bridge ever to be built across the Ohio River, and it was a National Road landmark for decades.

People in northern Virginia noted the success of the federal and state highways. Soon they were clamoring for a turnpike of their own to go cross-country from Winchester to Parkersburg and scale the humps of the Alleghenies in its course. Like the Kanawha Pike, this route had first been advocated by George Washington. Col. Claude Crozet, who had engineered battlements for Napoleon's army, was chosen by Virginia in 1831 to lay out this rugged path of progress. Later he became its overall construction supervisor.

The main bridges for this Northwestern Turnpike were designed by Lewis Wernwag, and plans and specifications flowed in a steady stream from the hand of the celebrated old master then living on his island at Harpers Ferry. Actual construction appears to have been sublet to Wernwag's trusted sons and his chief foremen. Covered wooden spans were soon in process of erection over the South and North Branches of the Potomac, the Cheat and Tygart's Valley Rivers, the West Fork of the Monongahela and Middle Island Creek.

The ends of the new pike were open in 1836 and in another year all the bridges were finished. Until the coming of the railroad, the Northwestern was traveled heavily both by westbound settlers and by cattle and produce coming east to seaboard markets. Sizable settlements grew up at all but one crossing, and some, like Grafton and Clarksburg, became first-class cities.

Colonel Crozet's curves and grades over the mountains were so well-engineered that little improvement could be made on them when the Northwestern Turnpike emerged from relative obscurity to carry auto traffic as U.S. 50. And two of the old covered bridges were still standing.

One was a landmark over Middle Island Creek at West Union which had served the county seat for well over a hundred years. Honorably "retired" in 1941 and used only for pedestrian traffic, it seemed to have good chances of lasting another century. Unhappily, during a freshet in June of 1950 it was washed off its foundations and slammed against its concrete successor on U.S. 50. Next day the West Virginia Road Commission dynamited the hulk to relieve pressure on the new span. The last of West Union Bridge went floating in chunks down swollen Middle Island Creek.

Back over the mountains on the old Northwestern stands the Cheat River Bridge. It is the only river crossing on the pike that still retains its rural atmosphere. The Caledonia

*Handsome West Union Bridge couldn't be saved.*

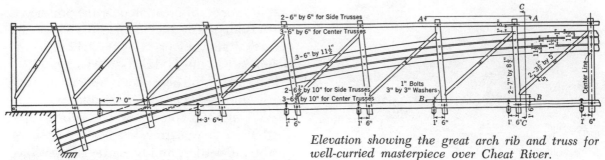

2-6" by 6" for Side Trusses
3-6" by 6" for Center Trusses
3-6" by 11½"
7' 0"
2-6½" by 10" for Side Trusses
3-6½" by 10" for Center Trusses
1" Bolts
3" by 3" Washers
2-7" by 8½"
2-3½" by 5"
Center Line
3' 6"    1' 6"    1' 6"    1' 6"    1' 6"C    1' 6"

*Elevation showing the great arch rib and truss for well-curried masterpiece over Cheat River.*

*Peace for Wernwag's only survivor.*

Tavern is no more, but in its day it welcomed many a wayfaring stranger in the shadow of the bridge. Its proprietor, Charles Hooten, doubled as toll collector. Some months his own take for the job ran as high as $150.

Cheat River is a big two-span, two-lane masterpiece of covered wooden bridge building, unused since 1932 but maintained as a "State relic." The legend on the portal says that it was built in 1835, but it is quite certain that this crossing was not completed until at least two years later. Its wonderful double arches and expert bracing bear the unmistakable trademarks of its designer, Lewis Wernwag. Construction was sublet to Josiah Kidwell, who received $18,000 for the job. It is the last example of Wernwag's work in existence today. Hugged by the escarpments of its lonely mountain valley and guarded by a huge sycamore, Cheat River Bridge today is a favorite picnic spot for travelers on the twisting old pike.

When the Northwestern was finished, Colonel Crozet laid out one more turnpike for the Commonwealth of Virginia before he turned to building railroads for a living. This was the Staunton & Parkersburg, a third and

middle route across the mountains to answer the pleas sent to the Virginia Legislature by mountain and valley settlers.

All the main river crossings of the center section of this turnpike were originally built by stern, raw-boned Lemuel Chenoweth, West Virginia's most prominent covered bridge builder. This man has become a legend in the state and his fame was richly deserved.

Born and raised in Virginia, Chenoweth lived in the vicinity of Beverly (now West Virginia) all his life. Educational opportunities in Randolph County were mighty meager. Young Lem attended "pauper schools"—paid for by state penalties and fines—which were seldom in session more than two months at a time. Chenoweth always gave a lot of credit for his knowledge to the reading of his Bible, and his imaginative flair for calculation and his astute engineering were certainly God-given.

At first Lem made fine furniture and did cabinetwork in his own shop at Beverly. Another of his specialties was sturdy wagons, which were in great demand throughout the mountains. Then the notices seeking bidders on state bridges began to intrigue the Beverly carpenter. It is little wonder a man of such competence should turn to bigger things in the building line; and he had a family of thirteen to provide for.

The story of how Lemuel Chenoweth won the contract for bridges on the Staunton & Parkersburg Turnpike in 1850 has several versions and bids fair to become a classic West Virginia folk tale. The account given by

LEMUEL CHENOWETH

Chenoweth's great-granddaughter, Mrs. Virginia Downey of Beverly, West Virginia, is perhaps the best.

The contractor had already built some small covered bridges in the vicinity of Weston, and a large one at Beverly, so he had a pretty good idea of the most effective truss plans on the market. Chenoweth put in some features of his own and constructed a plain wooden model, using the Burr arch as a basis; it was a knockdown framework which could easily be carried in his saddlebags. Then he set out on the dusty two-hundred-mile ride over the Blue Ridge to Richmond.

The Board of Public Works of the Commonwealth was already considering the bridge bids when the long-haired country cabinet-maker arrived in the capital. Fetching his wooden model pieces, Lem waited patiently while many types of bridges were shown and explained by their designers and promoters. There were wooden truss models on every current plan—iron structures, stone arches, wire cable suspensions, even a bridge of brick. The board members grew glassy-eyed and fidgety as the day wore on. Finally Chenoweth, as the last bidder, was asked if he wanted to submit his plans. For answer he took the wooden pieces he'd been holding and

quietly began to assemble them on a long table. Soon done, he placed his completed little span lightly on two chairs. Then he deliberately stood on his model and walked its length. As he stepped down he spoke his first words:

"Gentlemen, this is all I have to say!"

The authorities and engineers present were amazed and much impressed with Chenoweth's model and his confidence in its strength. Together with his submitted plans and low bid, this feat was doubtless responsible for his winning the five-bridge contract.

He was a busy man for a decade as he supervised the erection of his bridges on the Parkersburg and other smaller turnpikes in western Virginia. His peak year was 1852. With the aid of his brother Eli he put up a good wide arch bridge over Buffalo Creek at Barrackville while his Parkersburg Pike contracts were still not fully completed. Then he took on construction of what was to be his most famous monument, the big double-barreled Philippi Bridge over Tygart's Valley River.

Philippi Bridge as originally constructed by Chenoweth was of two spans, each 138 feet, 8 inches in the clear. The timber was yellow poplar, and the only metal used was in the form of iron bolts to hold the wooden segments together. The stone abutments and center pier were laid under the supervision of Emmett J. O'Brien, a master mason from Barbour County.

All the feverish building activity ground to a halt with the firing on Fort Sumter. Lemuel Chenoweth, a Southern sympathizer, had to sit out the conflict and see his careful handiwork shattered and burned in the fighting that raged up and down the valleys. We have already noted the part Philippi Bridge played in the War. Fortune smiled and brought it through a succession of invasions and guerilla raids, and it still stands today. A sidewalk and two new piers were added in 1934; the interior bracing was strengthened, and the old rounded portal entrances were squared off to

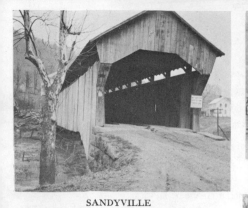

SANDYVILLE

BLUE SULPHUR SPRINGS

KINCHELO CREEK

ALDERSON

SINK'S MILL

WADESTOWN

CAMP COOLEY

CARROLLTON

INDIAN CREEK

ROMINE'S MILL

ROOTING CREEK

CAIRO

*Storied Philippi, despite rough time in War  (see also p. 31).*

accommodate higher stake-bodied trucks. In 1952 the bridge was given a hundredth birthday party complete with speeches, a pageant and all manner of gala festivities. The onetime carpenter would have been pleased to know his big bridge has stood up so well.

Chenoweth stayed pretty close to home after the War, puttering with inventions like a reverse-cutting sawmill and a means of laying underwater cable. His hometown bridge at Beverly had been burned in 1865. Seven years later Old Lem finally got around to replacing it with a duplicate which lasted until 1953. It was his final labor as the dean of West Virginia's covered bridge builders.

Today the Mountain State's covered bridges consist of a handful of outstanding structures like Philippi, Barrackville and Cheat River, plus a number of comparatively tiny backcountry spans.

Harrison County in the northern part of the state has the most, with ten remaining. At one time this county had over fifty roofed spans, big and little, and their history is recorded in Harvey W. Harmer's carefully compiled little *Covered Bridges of Harrison County, West*

*Page opposite—Twelve standing West Virginia bridges.*

*Virginia.* The great flood of July, 1888, did away with many of the important ones over the West Fork and its main tributaries, but some were replaced in kind. The present Romine's Mill Bridge, southeast of Clarksburg, was rebuilt in that year with timbers taken from a flood-wrecked covered structure over at West Milford. Using salvaged lumber saved a lot of money: the new bridge cost the county only $675.

In West Virginia the county courts once had the say on the building of bridges, and their minutes recorded the erection of covered ones. On receipt of a petition for a new bridge, the court would appoint a commissioner—often a prominent businessman with a bit of engineering training—who was empowered to contract for, and see to, the completion of the structure from streambed to rooftree.

Harrison County, for instance, appointed J. W. Hess to prepare plans and advertise for bids for a new bridge to be built at Margaret, a growing settlement just in the process of living down its original name of Hen Peck. Hess contracted in 1893 with J. J. Spencer and J. B. Wright to build the bridge for $529. It was only 32 feet long.

In the same year Spencer & Wright also put

up a 40-foot covered bridge over Tenmile Creek at Jarvisville, for which they received only $309. The bridge washed away in a freshet three years later. Stranded in a meadow some distance downstream, it was hauled back intact and replaced on its original abutments. There it still stands.

Half a dozen little covered bridges built in the 1880's and '90's for less than a thousand dollars are to be found in Monongalia County, close to the Pennsylvania line. Ritchie County has old Burr arch spans near Cairo and Berea, and there are five flood survivors on the upper reaches of West Fork in the vicinity of Weston.

Overwhelmed by the size and fame of the big Philippi structure a few miles away, an old covered bridge still clings to a precarious existence over the Buckhannon River at Carrollton. It is notable for its decorated portals, which were once brightly painted with complex geometrical figures and intertwined flowers as on a gaudy Pennsylvania barn.

Along the eastern mountain ranges are isolated little bridges near Dunmore, Alderson and Salt Sulphur Springs. And hard by the Kentucky border near Pritchard is the westernmost covered span in the state. Little bridges, yes, and of simple construction; but by virtue of the thoughtful addition of roofs they have served their West Virginia byroads far longer than their country-carpenter builders ever imagined was possible.

# THE DISTRICT OF COLUMBIA:
## Capital Crossings

FOR A CITY WHOSE HISTORY is as well documented as that of Washington, it is surprising to be able to learn so little of the covered bridges which once served the Capital. At one time there were three of them within the present limits of the District of Columbia, all stretching over the broad Potomac to Virginia.

On his trips from Mount Vernon to the old seat of government at Philadelphia, President George Washington habitually crossed the Potomac River by the Georgetown Ferry. Maj. Pierre Charles L'Enfant, who was at work planning the new capital, suggested to the President that Georgetown should have better communication with the south than was afforded by ferriage. "A bridge," urged M. L'Enfant passionately, "must span the Potomac!"

Soon the Georgetown Bridge Company was formed with an eye to serving the embryo Federal City. A building site was picked where the river narrowed at Little Falls (at the western corner of the present city of Washington) and many months were spent in erecting huge stone abutments on the banks. With all in readiness, the company sent for the man who was then America's leading bridge architect—Timothy Palmer of Newburyport, Massachusetts—to top the masonry with woodwork. The Yankee builder arrived in 1796 and proceeded to erect one of his trussed arch bridges, a gracefully curved single span with over-the-hill roadway. Although it included the identical truss principles of his later Permanent Bridge at Philadelphia, Palmer's 120-foot Little Falls Bridge at Georgetown was *not* a covered bridge.

George Washington never crossed a covered bridge, but he did use this first Potomac span at least once. In his diary for April 19, 1797, he recorded: "Went by the bridge at the little falls to Gt. Falls and returned in the afternoon." He noted that the charge for passage was "1s 10d"—sevenpence more than the ferry. Even the Father of his Country and the new nation's first ex-President was not exempt from rapacious tollgathering.

His Permanent Bridge converted Timothy Palmer to roofs and weatherboarding, and he

*Chain Bridge as it looked when a weary President inspected Union forts.*

wrote as much in 1806. But by that time it was too late to add a cover to Little Falls: although the builder was unaware of it, the structure had already decayed and collapsed. A duplicate succumbed to floodwaters in six months. The huge abutments constricted the river to such a degree in time of freshet that the Potomac boiled against the stonework, rising as much as thirty-seven feet in its frenzy to get through, and so tore away three successive bridges. The last was a pioneer of the suspension type with the roadway hung from long chains attached to wooden towers on the abutments. Called the Chain Bridge, it left its name to the modern crossing which leads from Canal to Leesburg Roads in Washington, N.W.

A real covered bridge was finally erected on the site after the open Chain Bridge was swept away in 1840. Not confined to a single span, the new Chain Bridge was of tough and taut Howe truss construction, with seven pairs of huge arches to strengthen it further. A narrow footwalk was attached to the upstream side of its 1,300-foot bulk.

The new Chain Bridge was the terminus of the Leesburg and Georgetown Pike, and so formed a strategic entrance to the Capital. During the Civil War it was heavily guarded day and night. The Chain Bridge "battery," consisting of two 12-pounders, was mounted in a barricade at the northern entrance, with the cannon trained to sweep any hot-headed storming of the bridge by Confederate raiders or Southern partisans. As a precaution against arson and sabotage the siding and the entire roof were removed. Abraham Lincoln often used Chain Bridge in his inspection trips to the twenty forts that protected the approaches to

the city. The bridge survived the conflict but was left in its denuded state until replaced in 1874.

Some five miles downstream, the second Potomac bridge to be built in the District once joined the foot of muddy Maryland Avenue to Alexander's Island on the Virginia shore. The filled land of East Potomac Park did not exist in 1809, and the pile-and-trestle bridge erected in that year stretched for nearly a mile across the broad reaches of the Potomac. It was easy to give the lonely, wind-swept structure the name by which the crossing was always to be called: Long Bridge.

Theodore Burr had traveled down from his one-time home in New York State to be an unsuccessful bidder on this bridge. If he had snagged the original contract, Washington would almost certainly have had a series of noble soaring arches in the grand manner of the McCall's Ferry giant and Harrisburg's Camelback Bridge. As it was, the simple wooden roadway stuck on piles above the mud flats suffered badly in times of high water.

Then there was the incident in 1814 when American forces burned the south end of the bridge to prevent the invading British army from crossing over. The British put the torch to the north end—just in spite—only to have the flames quenched in a sudden cloudburst which also helped save the unfinished capitol building and the White House. The Washington Bridge Company pampered and patched its property for twenty-two years. When an ice jam carried away a substantial portion of Long Bridge in 1831, the company directors considered themselves lucky to sell out their interest to the federal government for $20,000.

Grandiose plans for a new bridge were soon formulated by the Army Engineers: one was for a new iron bridge on stone piers and a second was for a crossing to be made entirely of stone. Either one would cost, they estimated, well over a million dollars. News of these schemes reached and ruffled Andrew Jackson in the White House. Old Hickory snorted that such expense would be a downright extravagance. He opined that a sturdy wooden bridge was entirely adequate; and, as watchdog of the public purse strings, he got his way.

In the end Congress appropriated $130,000 for a new structure comprising a 1,660-foot earth causeway on the shoals in midstream—an arrangement whereby a lot of bridging was eliminated—with a covered section at either end of it, and short open drawspans over the Virginia and Maryland (now Washington) Channels. Presumably the wooden sections were built on Col. Stephen H. Long's five-year-old panel truss plan, additionally appropriate in a bridge of this name (later this superstructure was rebuilt with heavier Howe trusses).

President Jackson and his Cabinet walked the exposed and weary mile to open the new Long Bridge officially on October 1, 1835. A fall gale whitecapped the Potomac as the President made his way over what he must have

felt was a sensible piece of engineering. Happily, someone thought to provide a carriage for the party's return.

Like Chain Bridge upstream, Long Bridge was unhoused and heavily guarded during the Civil War. Its defenders even removed whole sections of plank flooring at night to discourage unauthorized passage. Soon, to speed troop movements, railroad tracks were laid on a portion of the highway and carried their first trains in 1862. Later a separate wooden railroad bridge was built alongside. On February 18, 1865, twenty-nine and a half tons of freight train, including the engine *Vibard*, crunched through the south spans of this bridge. The *Vibard* was rescued but the bridge was considered unsafe. The railroad company then tacked another separate lane onto the old Long Bridge, with the center truss serving to keep market-bound farm wagons from Virginia off the tracks.

Long Bridge does not appear to have ever been re-roofed and re-sided after the Civil War. Thousands of people and hundreds of vehicles traveled it daily, yet it survived their passage and the work of the elements, plus the damage done by no less than nine floods. Steel spans did not replace the exposed and creaking wooden trusses until 1906.

Like the other two bridges of the nation's

*Wartime photo shows stripped Long Bridge, far left; details of its railroad twin at right.*

*It was no trick for canal boat in foreground to cross Ithiel Town's Aqueduct Bridge.*

Capital, the Aqueduct Bridge was not originally a covered structure, but became one.

Cocky little Ithiel Town, architect and bridge promoter from Connecticut, maintained an office in Washington during Jackson's time. Although he was disappointed not to get the contract for rebuilding Long Bridge he soon had bigger fish to fry. The newly-formed Alexandria Canal Company wished to span the Potomac with an aqueduct for their extension of the Chesapeake & Ohio Canal. The company's directors hired Ithiel Town as their bridge consultant.

Jacksonian Democracy had been niggardly with its appropriation for the public's Long Bridge. However, the treasury coffers were opened when it came to helping the canal company: $450,000 was contributed toward erecting the new aqueduct at Georgetown. Andy Jackson must have been asleep during that session.

The canalers would have preferred an all-stone structure but they settled for one with stone piers carrying a trussed wooden trunk. Town and his partner, Alexander J. Davis, built them a good bridge to enclose the waterway,

using Town's patent lattice "mode" of construction. The result was 1,446 feet long in nine spans, with the heavy wooden trough 17 feet wide and 7 feet deep. Always in evidence were continual jets of water spurting from it here and there, for no wooden aqueduct ever built was entirely leakproof. One wag always referred to its angular bulk as the "punctured dragon of the Potomac."

For thirty years the Georgetown Aqueduct carried coal- and lumber-laden canal boats from Cumberland, Paw Paw and Point of Rocks down to tidewater at Alexandria. Then Civil War brought emergency changes. The waterlogged flume was drained to provide a roadway for Union troops deployed to protect the Capital.

After the War the aqueduct became a rare type of covered bridge—combining canal and highway on two levels. The superstructure was entirely rebuilt in 1866 on the more modern Howe truss plan, to which were added arches fashioned with five thicknesses of timber. The builders put the canal and towpath between trusses and laid out a top-story roadway with high railings along the flat roof. For twenty years the strollers of Washington and the carriages of Congressmen and their ladies made the wide top planking of Georgetown Aqueduct a well-traveled promenade of a Sunday afternoon. Below them the mules plodded along and boatmen guided their boats through the dim watery passage high above the Potomac. One elderly canaler recalls the time when, as a small boy on the towpath of Georgetown Aqueduct, he peered up and first learned that ladies had feet—and ankles!

In 1886 the government purchased the crossing; the canal was abandoned and a new iron truss bridge was built on the site. The ruins of the old piers can still be seen in the river west of the present Francis Scott Key Bridge.

Engineering historians who visit Washing-

*New Georgetown aqueduct still sprayed the Potomac, offered quick course in anatomy.*

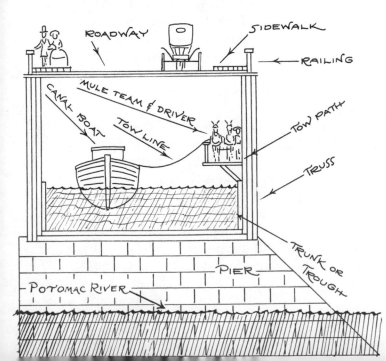

ton usually make straight for the records of the United States Patent Office, where one can see primary source material on who invented what bridge and how it really looked. Unfortunately all the records prior to 1836 were destroyed by fire, along with the little wooden models required to represent each design. Skillfully, from other sources, many of the drawings and patent specifications have been restored. They make a fascinating study. Here are the original designs of builders whose inventions dotted the Middle Atlantic landscape, of men like Burr, Wernwag, Town, Long, Hassard and Haupt.

As we know, Timothy Palmer got a patent for his truss, but its exact details are unknown today. The first drawing that shows a roof and weatherboarding is included, almost as an afterthought, with the designs of Thomas Pope of New York City, whose patent for a "flying pendent lever bridge" was issued April 18, 1807.

Pope was also the first man in America to publish a full-sized book about bridges. His *Treatise on Bridge Architecture*, which appeared in 1811, gives a history of bridges up to that time, and also extolls the virtues of Pope's own creation. With it he hoped to conquer the East River at New York with a single mighty wooden arch of 1,800 feet or more! The "flying bridge" is explained in detail, but of the visionary patentee we know only from a contemporary source that he was an architect and landscape gardener, a good draftsman and "a respectable man with a large and expensive family."

Of the fifty-one patents issued for wooden bridges from 1797 to 1860 less than a dozen acquired any real popularity. Among the records are the plans of men just as sincere in purpose as the more practical and successful patentees. Like the admirable Mr. Pope's brain child, however, their bridge building schemes seem laughable today.

Early in 1841 Messrs. Price and Philips of Golden, Maryland, patented a "puzzle-keyed

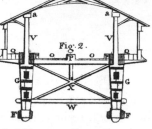

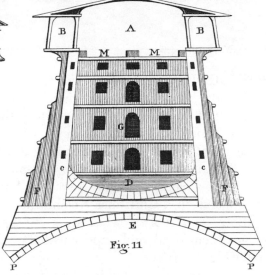

bridge" based frankly on a child's toy wherein the last piece of a little wooden puzzle supported and locked all the rest in place. The problem was to hold the all-but-completed span together until that final key timber could be inserted. Later the same year Isaiah Rogers of New York patented a "spiral-braced cylinder bridge." It was a round tube of wooden strips curved and interwoven to enclose the roadway, and vaguely resembled a king-size squirrel trap.

A patent was issued in 1843 to John R. Remington for a new kind of coffeepot. Presumably Remington needed the coffee for the mental energy to dream up his next patent, an airy cantilever-type wooden bridge (not covered) with a deliberate sag in the middle. The inventor dubbed it Remington's Wonderful Bridge and built one in Alabama with the tremendous length of 436 feet. It actually stood over a ravine for a short while before tumbling down, taking the inventor's dreams of fame and riches along with it.

Some patentees were "combiners"—men who took the best features of others' plans and combined them as their own. The acme for bridges of this type was reached by one Ammi White of Boston. His patent of February 3, 1852, calls for a wooden suspension bridge with laminated timber "cables." He enclosed his bridge tightly except for the towers, which stuck out like masts from the top of his contraption. Then, aping the English square-beamed iron bridges just coming into prominence, he called his a "tubular truss bridge." Apparently Ammi was

bent on getting aboard *all* the bridge building bandwagons.

For a while the Patent Office kept and displayed its models, including those of bridges. The fire of 1836 had taken all the early ones, and another conflagration in 1877 destroyed eighty thousand others sent in during forty-odd years to illustrate every aspect of American inventiveness. Models are no longer required for the issuance of a patent and what remained of the former collection has been dispersed

It is therefore highly gratifying that the Smithsonian Institution's Division of Mechanical & Civil Engineering is in the process of having nearly sixty models constructed to show America's progress in bridge building from 1797 to the present. The models, many of them large and elaborate, will be exhibited in a new hall to be completed in 1962. Thus, although the famed Chain and Long Bridges and the old "punctured dragon" aqueduct are long gone, visitors soon will be able to see their designs in model form, and to study the trusses that held them in place above the Potomac when our Capital was young.

# VI

# Memories for Tomorrow

MOST RESIDENTS of the Middle Atlantic States have known well or can recall at least one covered bridge, and with little effort they can see it now in their mind's eye: old and weatherbeaten certainly, and quiet; a cool place to stand and dream on a lazy Summer's day, or a welcome shelter from the bitter North wind on a Christmas tree-hunting expedition. The roof is what does it. Open bridges seem bleak and impersonal; the covered bridge is a friend.

The friendship is rooted in a hundred years of service. Stop by the gaunt and empty abutments where a covered bridge once stood, look beyond the stretch of overgrowth that used to be the turnpike and picture the thoroughfare in its heyday. Plodding oxen, Conestoga wagons with their tinkling bells, sheep and geese on their way to market—then a horn in the distance and the rush and rattle of the

Pittsburgh stage. All travelers had to pause and cross the palm of the wizened tollgatherer before he'd raise the gate to let them pass on, from the choking dust of the road into the cool shadows of the long bridge. It was a time when the people went West to the bountiful new lands where corn grew high and hogs fat. Then East would come their products to the markets of Philadelphia, Baltimore and Richmond.

The covered bridge was a big factor in making this vast inland commerce possible. Ferries and fords were to be avoided; the toll roads required and built bridges of wood, with roofs. There was music in the names of streams these bridges spanned for the turnpikes—Octoraro, Conewago, Tuscarora; Gunpowder, Cacapon, Gauley and Cheat. Restless wheels beat a rhythm across the thumping planks of the floors as whole families passed through the far portals and never looked back.

Later, with the coming of canal and railroad, the pikes languished, went broke and lay moribund for nearly a century. Only here and there where a living could be eked out did a bridge remain in the care of a tollgatherer. It was considered great sport to wait just out of sight until the collector was otherwise engaged, and then "run" the bridge with a whoop and holler. Horses could usually outdistance a man in the race for the barrier. The outrage stamped on the keeper's face was reward enough.

"You run my bridge!" he'd yell, fists waving as he hopped up and down. "You run my bridge! I'll——I'll——"

But whatever dire threats he uttered would

OUT OUR WAY —By Williams

FUN? WHAT KIND OF FUN? A GUY MUST HAVE BEEN SIMPLE-MINDED TO HAVE FUN AROUND A HOLLOW SHELL LIKE THAT!

WE HAD TO MAKE OUR OWN FUN--WE DIDN'T HAVE EVERY-THING MADE FOR US--WE HAD TO THINK!

OOH! THEY'RE OFF FOR THE REST OF THE TRIP!

BORN THIRTY YEARS TOO SOON 2-18 J.R.WILLIAMS

be lost in a clatter of hoofs and a blinding swirl of dust.

Back on the side roads that branched from main pikes they built covered bridges too, until a good many villages each had its own well-made span. Such bridges took on the flavor of the towns they served.

In the East they were more prim, kept painted a fresh red or white and scrupulously whitewashed inside. Signs on either portal warned travelers to WALK YOUR HORSES OR PAY FIVE DOLLARS. Often a POST NO BILLS proclamation was in evidence, enforced by a constable with his weather eye peeled for characters up to no good. Later on the town fathers might add a sidewalk which became a promenade for even the old folks on a soft Spring night. Then care was taken to keep the lamps filled and shining balefully on this part of the bridge, lest footpads spring from the darkness to accost those late in going home.

In the newer counties to the West, with their boom towns of falsefront and bustle, the covered spans were usually rather battered. Boro councils were too harried to get them painted and drummers were free to plaster them with signs. Advertisements for Clabber Girl Baking Powder, Neat's-foot Oil, Bull Durham Plug and Pearline Soap were emblazoned in many colors and combinations to edify the passers-by. Often the town gallants would lounge in the shelter of an entrance and a poor working girl, her cheeks burning, had to run the gantlet of their remarks. Sometimes the North End boys would stage a donnybrook in the no man's land of the village bridge, taking on the South Enders with fists

and siding torn from the protesting walls, all for the sheer joy of battle.

A country bridge was another thing entirely. Here was quiet, with only an occasional rig clattering over. Boys and girls, traipsing home from school, could dally away a half-hour of chore time in a familiar bridge. One could always toss pebbles into the pool below, watch spiders and phoebes, carve initials or read other scribblings aloud in innocence.

One West Virginia youth made a profitable thing of waiting out a thunderstorm in a covered bridge. He was clambering among the rafters when he came upon a dusty cache of gold coins and jewelry, presumably hidden by a robber who couldn't return for his loot. Another boy heard of the treasure find and determined to search every covered bridge he crossed. Patience paid off. One day, at last, his exploring fingers closed around something stuffed into a cranny under the eaves of a remote little span. Scarcely able to believe his luck, he pulled forth a thick wad of—Confederate bills.

A Marylander tells of the good use a certain country bridge not far from town was put to long ago. The young people were, of course, not permitted to dance on the Sabbath. Nevertheless they hit upon a workable scheme for Sunday evenings. A group would take a fiddle or two and repair to the covered bridge for a hymn-sing. There they took turns singing while some of the others circled and dipped in forbidden revelry. The boys and girls literally had themselves a ball, and nobody within hearing of the bridge seemed to notice that the hymns were rendered in three-quarter time.

*Old Hunsecker's Mill Bridge in Lancaster County, Penna., stirs romance of tourism, hikes gas consumption.*

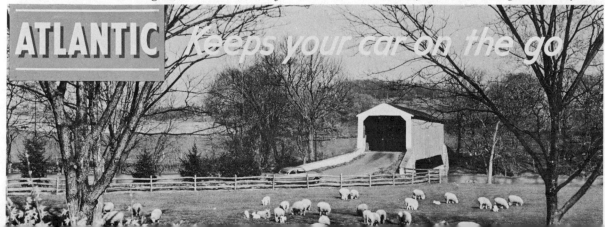

ATLANTIC *keeps your car on the go*

It is presumed that the dancers first swept out their ballroom's floor, for covered spans could have a mighty pungent odor. An old Virginia expression described a very poor grade of pipe fillings. "That's covered bridge tobacco," someone would snort; "half manure and half splinters!"

Not all memories of these spans are gentle ones. Covered bridges could be scary places, especially at night when roofs and siding made the darkness inside a lonesome crossing even blacker, and every half-seen shadow seemed to be a giant with a club or an old hag with clawing hands. Local legends attribute many remote timbered tunnels with being the favorite spots for robbery and even murder. Pennsylvania author Cornelius Weygandt tells of his Uncle Jim who, while crossing the Norristown Bridge one night, stepped right smack on a recumbent cow. The beast rose up, so did Jim, and so did his hair. Although he'd been at Antietam, and Gettysburg, too, he claimed that his scare in the bridge was about the worst he'd ever had in his life.

Such are the tales of the Middle Atlantic region's covered bridges. Handed down and embellished to become part of national folklore, they are linked with a time when life was less frenetic and unknown dangers were things as easily definable as a sleeping cow in a bridge. Yet, as we have seen, many of the old structures have not gone the way of our vanished past. That these fine examples of American engineering are still standing is a tribute to their own integrity and, in a number of cases, to the public spirit of individuals and groups working to preserve them. We have already noted the pride Philippi, West Virginia, takes in its famous covered bridge and the efforts of the Covington, Virginia, professional women to assure Old Humpback's continued life. The by–passed Cheat River Bridge in West Virginia, and South Side Virginia's Marysville Bridge continue to elicit "oh's" and "ah's" from passengers as cars start to dash by and then slow up alongside.

However, still far too few people think very hard about saving a familiar landmark until its removal is an accomplished fact. Pennsylvania, always rich in covered bridges, did not seem to be in much danger of losing them until recent years. As the hand of Time picked off bridge after bridge, folks in the Boros and townships would say: "Well, Elmer's Bridge is gone, but we still have Huff's and Yahn's." Then suddenly came the day when Huff's and Yahn's were only piles of wood beside new concrete bridges.

Pennsylvania's vast state highway system is responsible for maintaining more than a hun-

THE OLD HOMESTEAD. BENJAMIN DAWSON & BRO. OIL FARM. OHIO TP. P.O. SMITHS FERRY, PA.

dred covered bridges. For these the future is bleak. The highway department sees only to repairs that are absolutely necessary, and makes no bones about desiring to tear down these spans as soon as funds are appropriated to replace them. Any bridge posted for less than 15 tons of weight and 14 feet clearance in height is already on the drafting boards to be replaced in the state's long-range plan. The target date for completing the program has been set as 1962, but it appears improbable that all the one hundred and twenty bridges owned by the state will have replacements by then. Officially though, they are on borrowed time, and any photographer of covered bridges who plans to visit the Keystone Commonwealth would do best to corral the state bridges first. They are indicated as such on our Pennsylvania roster which appears in Appendix II. Have a look at old Loux's Bridge in Bucks County before all the shingles blow off; Amwake's Mill in Lancaster County before it outsags its supports, and Paisley Bridge in Greene County before it becomes an absolute skeleton.

In recent years Pennsylvania covered bridges have suffered from a rash of senseless burnings that seems to be headed toward epidemic proportions. The pattern is getting to be shockingly familiar. There will be a small minority of residents who want a new bridge,

*Guaranteed Rx for extermination: arson and neglect dispose of Liesz's (below) and Spring Garden.*

claiming that a perfectly sound wooden structure is "outmoded." State and county officials, laudably slow to spend the public's money to soothe the esthetic reactions of only a few, demur and delay. All too often of late the next step is told in big black headlines: COVERED BRIDGE BURNS—ARSON SUSPECTED. The minority, through one or two ruthless individuals, has forced the issue.

In this manner Shaw's and Brinton's Bridges in Chester County went up in flames. Worthington's Mill Bridge in Bucks County and Liesz's Bridge in Berks both succumbed to mysterious blazes, and the burning of Eyster's Bridge, Pennsylvania's longest, on St. Patrick's Day, 1958, climaxed an all-too-frequent series of bridge fires of "unknown cause."

So long as the covered bridges are safe and strong, the answer to such vandalism is to instill local pride in the residents who live near them and use them, to hammer home the facts

concerning the historical and engineering values of these structures. Toward this end a new chapter of the National Society for the Preservation of Covered Bridges was formed at Harrisburg in the Spring of 1959. Led by three veteran Pennsylvania champions of the "embattled relics"—Mrs. Vera H. Wagner, Henry Falk and George R. Wills—the organization, now independent, is aptly named for Theodore Burr. It proposes to help preserve, commemorate and record historical facts concerning the Keystone State's covered bridges, both past and present. Members will meet, take field trips, and act as a unit to insure the continued existence of notable Pennsylvania spans. The Connecticut River Valley Covered Bridge Society, a New England group with national membership, has already run two successful excursions to visit the remaining spans in eastern Pennsylvania, and expects to enlarge its field in the future.

These organizations are an outgrowth of mounting interest in covered bridges, which paradoxically seems to increase as the number of bridges decreases. Through the years dozens of people have realized that there were a great many covered crossings in the Middle Atlantic area to see and record on film. Individuals have roamed the countryside from Delaware Bay to the Ohio River and south to the Carolinas, searching, snapping pictures and recording statistics and history. Some, in battered cars and armed with maps, cameras and dogged determination, have visited and photographed every covered bridge in the area. Others specialize in only one state, or in a particular county or region.

Mr. and Mrs. Harold L. Sitler, and their three young sons and daughter, show what

can be accomplished in the line of covered bridge research. Beginning in early 1954, this family from Hershey, Pennsylvania, set out systematically to visit and photograph every covered bridge in the state. There were over four hundred at the time, many of them far off the beaten tracks and unlisted by either state or county agencies. The Sitlers toured weekends and holidays on a limited budget, with picnic fare at roadside stops. They covered thousands of miles and took a little over two years to finish the job. As a result this family has a complete and priceless record in color of every Pennsylvania covered bridge in existence. And they'll still drive a hundred miles or more to check on a rumor of one they might have missed.

Despite the prospect of wholesale replace-

**All in a Lifetime    -:-    Recollections**

LOVERS' LANE — THROUGH THE OLD COVERED BRIDGE.

*South Perkasie inched along for eight days.*

ment, an occasional loss from high water, and the infamous bridge burnings, the picture for preservation is not completely dark. In 1958 it came time to replace the 126-year-old South Perkasie Bridge in Bucks County, Pennsylvania. The few local people who wanted to save the structure despaired of finding the means to do it. Andrew Schuler, head of the Perkasie Historical Society, saw little hope, but he wouldn't give up. He wrote letters, pleaded with officials and talked to the contractor for the new concrete crossing. Then he launched his final try: a drive to raise more than $4000 to move the old lattice bridge to a new site. For this amount Schuler inveigled the contractor into raising the historic relic off its abutments and carrying it on fork-lift trucks to Lenape Park a mile away. This method of moving the span was feasible because the crisscrossed timbers of Town's design allowed the structure to be braced and held as tight as a box for its journey, and so it traveled far better than a bridge built with any other truss type would have done.

What the contractor, E. A. Gallagher & Son of Philadelphia, may have lost in time and wages was more than made up by favorable publicity. Thousands of people converged on Perkasie during the eight days it took to move the bridge. They made bets on whether or not its 85-foot bulk could be wedged around the corner of Main and Walnut Streets in the Boro, but the bridge swung the angle with feet to spare. There was no real trouble al-

though progress was slow, and the old span now rests safely in its new park surroundings.

Then there is the story of Mrs. Margaret Wister Meigs. Not only did Mrs. Meigs like old covered bridges, she determined to own one. Luckily, as owner of the Fort Hunter Museum north of Harrisburg, Pennsylvania, she had a place to put it. Mrs. Meigs accomplished the moving of her bridge in a somewhat different manner from the one employed at South Perkasie. She simply went out and bought an unused covered bridge from the Pennsylvania State Highway Department—a span across Little Buffalo Creek in Perry County some eighteen miles from Fort Hunter.

The structure had to be taken down, transported and put up again. This task was performed by a middle-aged carpenter; his young helper, who was scared to death to climb up on the bridge; a farmer, and an elderly handyman. This unlikely quartet took about a month to accomplish the removing and the rebuilding, "aided by block and tackle and an old gray mare." Today the bridge stands mounted on dry land just inside the entrance to the museum. It is a monument to the great deal only a few individuals can do in the way of covered bridge preservation.

bridge. It is a nice little 23-footer, painted red, over a tributary of the South Branch of the Patapsco River on his farm near Woodbine, Maryland.

Back up in Monroe County, Pennsylvania —which hadn't had a covered bridge in years— the flood of 1955 washed out a stone bridge on the grounds of Mr. and Mrs. Richard Bullock's Swiftwater Inn at Swiftwater. Under the guidance of an architect and friend, E. Kenny Crothers, the Bullocks had a fine new covered bridge placed over Swiftwater Creek. An eye-catching addition to the inn, this is Pennsylvania's newest covered bridge. You can be sure that it won't be the last.

Others who admire the virtues of covered spans have built their own bridges from scratch. In 1952, just a few miles from the heart of busy Philadelphia, Robert H. Smith threw a covered bridge 16 feet, 6 inches long over a small stream beside his house and saw-mill near Manoa. It cost $850, but Mr. Smith figures that his little crossing will outlast half a dozen open wooden bridges.

Earlier, Hubert P. Burdette, a real estate man in Mount Airy, Maryland, had entertained much the same idea. A whimsical remark that he'd "always wanted a cigar-store Indian and a covered bridge," prompted somebody to give him one of the painted wooden effigies. Then he felt duty-bound to build the

With their interesting settings and unique forms of construction, covered bridges should be allowed to stand and be used wherever it is possible and practical for them to do so. Champions of the picturesque, like the far-sighted people already referred to, are hard at work toward this end. However, it is not just age or historical importance that entitles our roofed spans to preservation. On secondary roads, given proper care and maintenance, a covered bridge is still today a logical, economical and efficient structure.

*Fort Hunter Bridge, above left, was moved eighteen miles to present site. Others are newly built: Smith's Saw-mill and Burdette, above center and right; Swiftwater and Knoebel's Grove footbridge.*

# APPENDIX I – WHAT MAKES A BRIDGE

The following is a summary of two chapters from *Covered Bridges of the Northeast*, published in 1957 as the first volume in a projected series on America's great wooden bridges and their builders. R. S. A.

A bridge is defined simply as a structure erected to furnish a roadway over a depression or an obstacle; that is, over valleys or chasms, over water or other roads.

In general, bridges are supported in four ways: they are 1) propped from below—as by piling or trestles bedded in the bottom of a river or a defile; 2) carried for short distances by their own rigidity—as by stout logs, steel girders or prestressed concrete slabs; 3) held by the action of triangular (plus sometimes curved) arrangements of wooden or metal members, pressing against themselves as they press against land masses—as by trusses, or 4) hung from towers or upward projecting land masses—as in suspension bridges.

This book is concerned with the third classification, that of *truss* bridges. To understand them, though, it is necessary to start with the simple *stringer* crossings of the first group.

Man's first bridge was a stringer: he simply felled a tree growing on a riverbank so that it spanned the gap to the opposite bank. Then he teetered across it. Later he refined his invention by placing another log parallel to the first one and laying billets of wood across both of them to form a wider walkway, thus:

But what if a stream was wide? The longer the logs, the more likely they were to sag. The answer, developed centuries ago in Central Europe, was to cut two logs, press their butts into the banks (the shore foundations, called *abutments*) so that they met at an obtuse angle under the midpoint of the stringers; these were *braces*. Later a parallel stringer was added to close the open side of the triangle and keep the arms of the braces from shifting. The new stringer below was called the *lower chord*; the original one was the *upper chord*.

This combination of chords and braces was the first truss: a triangular system of timbers so devised that each member helped to support another, and together they supported whatever weight was put upon the whole.

Bridge building developed with piecemeal innovations during the Dark Ages, culminating in a virtually slipproof support when a centerpost was introduced to reach from the apex of the triangle to the midpoint of the lower chord, and so form this *kingpost* truss:

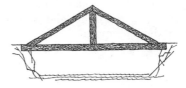

The kingpost was the earliest formal bridge truss design and it employed a primary engineering principle: a triangle will hold its shape under a load until its side members or its joints are crushed.

It is well to stop here and emphasize that the actual bridge consists of two trusses, one on each side; therefore the roadway—and, in covered spans, the roof and weatherboarding—has little to do with the bridge's basic structural efficiency. The description can be streamlined further by the reasonable practice of including the two sides in referring to the truss of a bridge.

The first kingpost truss was built under the stringers (forming a *deck* truss), where it was highly vulnerable to flood and ice. Then some inspired builder realized that kingpost triangles were equally effective when erected above the stringers (making a *through* truss). This rather oversimplified diagram and its explanation tell why:

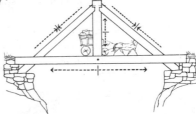

Although seemingly inelastic, the diagonal braces—called *compression members*—are subjected to squeeze as a load passes over the bridge. Meanwhile the same native flexibility allows the centerpost and lower chord —the *tension members*—to be pulled downward. So, if its truss is abutted properly into the banks, a bridge shoves harder against the land with the more weight that is put upon it, and the interaction of its truss members actually makes it stronger when it carries a load.

The whole matter of shifts and variations in stress is extremely complex and wasn't described fully until 1847. By then the wooden truss had undergone many elaborations.

A natural development was this *queenpost* truss, in which the peak of the kingpost triangle was replaced by a horizontal crosspiece to allow the base to be longer and span wider streams:

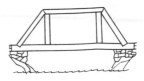

The next amplification produced the even longer *multiple kingpost,* a series of uprights with all braces inclined toward the centerpost:

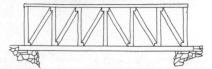

A river that was neither too swift nor too deep could be crossed by supporting such an elongated truss with one or more natural or man-made piers rising from the streambed. In a *multi-span* bridge of this sort the number of spans is one more than the number of intermediate supports between abutments.

Still, sometimes the character of a river made piers impossible: then a corollary design was used which combined an arch with a multiple kingpost. The earliest known drawings of the basic multiple kingpost and arch combinations were published in 1570 by Andrea Palladio. By that time, too, builders had begun to side and roof their bridges, simply to prevent the wooden trusses from rotting.

From the mid-1500's until the nineteenth century wooden bridge design lay dormant. Then came America's trio of pioneer builders—Palmer, Burr and Wernwag—to use the arch and kingpost for spans of a size hitherto undreamed of.

Timothy Palmer's design, patented in 1797, had auxiliary trusswork digging deep into the face of the abutments below the braced double arch:

PALMER

This was his general plan for the nation's first covered bridge, finished at Philadelphia in 1805.

A year earlier, Theodore Burr had patented this arch-truss:

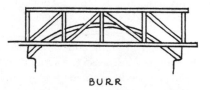

BURR

Each of its sides was a great arch sandwiched between two conventional kingpost arrangements, and its roadway, unlike Palmer's, was level. Burr used this plan for his all-time record single span (360' 4") at McCall's Ferry, Pennsylvania.

Flared kingposts bracing a double arch were the hallmarks of the best of Lewis Wernwag's many designs, which began with The Colossus in 1812. The one most popularly accepted looked like this:

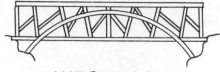

WERNWAG

A wholly American truss plan appeared in 1820, ideal for cheap, strong bridges that were easy to build. It was this "lattice mode" by Ithiel Town:

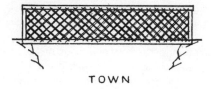

TOWN

Merely a series of overlapping triangles with no arches or uprights, it resembled a crisscross garden fence that could be "built by the mile and cut off by the yard" to support spans up to 200 feet in length. It was his new approach to the use of the basic unadorned triangle that made Town's truss unique.

A decade later Col. Stephen H. Long introduced this panel truss, a series of boxed X's with three or more panels comprising the entire truss:

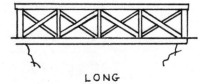

LONG

In 1840 William Howe brought about a bridge building revolution by introducing an iron rod into wooden trusses. Howe's design unabashedly copied the Long panel, replacing its uprights with iron tie-rods that could be readily adjusted with nuts and turnbuckles:

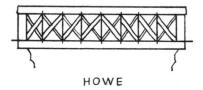

HOWE

Thus he coped with the major weakness of wood in bridge construction: the elasticity which allows strength-giving compression also permits the joints of an upright tension member to pull apart under heavy loads.

The Howe truss became the favored railroad bridge across America, and even influenced bridge construction in Europe and Asia. With it, wooden bridge building reached its peak; and with it the transition was made to bridges built of iron and steel.

# APPENDIX II. TABULATION OF EXISTING COVERED BRIDGES

This list, which omits foot bridges, is otherwise as accurate and complete as I have been able to make it. Still, there will be additions and corrections; for any such information I shall be grateful. R. S. A. June 1, 1959. SYMBOLS IN TABLE: K-P (Kingpost), Q-P (Queenpost), MK-P (Multiple Kingpost), A (Adapted), Ar (Arched), P (Private), T (State); TB (Twin Bridges).

## DELAWARE

| LOCATION | NAME | OWN-ER | STREAM | SPANS & LENGTH | DATE | TYPE | BUILDER, ETC. |
|---|---|---|---|---|---|---|---|
| **NEWCASTLE COUNTY** | | | | | | | |
| W of Ashland | Ashland Mill | | Red Clay Creek | 1- | | Town | |
| S of Ashland | | | Red Clay Creek | 1- | | Town | Abandoned |
| Wooddale | | | Red Clay Creek | 1- | | Town | Built on Skew |
| NE of Granogue | Smith's | T | Brandywine Creek | 1-154' | 1839 | Burr | Two Auxil. Piers |

## MARYLAND

| LOCATION | NAME | OWN-ER | STREAM | SPANS & LENGTH | DATE | TYPE | BUILDER, ETC. |
|---|---|---|---|---|---|---|---|
| **BALTIMORE COUNTY** | | | | | | | |
| NW of Hereford | Bunker Hill | | Gunpowder Falls | 1- | 1880 | Burr | |
| **BALTIMORE-HARFORD COUNTIES** | | | | | | | |
| Jerusalem | | | Little Gunpowder Falls | 1- | c1880 | Burr | |
| **CECIL COUNTY** | | | | | | | |
| Bayview | Gilpin's | | Northeast Creek | 1- | c1860 | Burr | |
| NE of Fairhill | Foxcatcher Farms | P | Big Elk Creek | 1- | | Burr | on Wm duPont est. |
| **HOWARD COUNTY** | | | | | | | |
| SW of Woodbine | Burdette | P | Trib S Br Patapsco Riv | 1-24' | c1938 | Stringer | |
| **FREDERICK COUNTY** | | | | | | | |
| NE of Thurmont | Roddy | | Owens Creek | 1-40' | | K-P | |
| Loy's Station | Loy's | T | Owens Creek | 1- | | MK-P | Auxil. Pier Added |
| Utica Mills | | | Fishing Creek | 1- | 1889 | Burr | Auxil. Pier Added[1] |
| **ADAMS COUNTY** | | | | | | | |
| Beechersville[2] | | T | Conewago Creek | 1-89' | 1836 | Burr | |
| E of Plainview | Snyder's Fording | T | Conewago Creek | 2-158' | 1868 | Burr | J.M. Pittenturf & Bro. |
| NW of New Chester | Sharrer's Mill | T | Conewago Creek | 1-73' | | Burr | |
| SW of E Berlin | Kuhn's Fording | | Conewago Creek | 2-222' | | Burr | |
| SW of Berlin | Bear's Fording[3] | T | Conewago Creek | 2-190' | 1862 | Burr | Samuel Stouffer |
| SE of Centennial | Dellone's Mill | | S Br Conewago Creek | 1-54' | 1850 | Burr | Henry Chritzman[4] |
| NE of Centennial | | T | S Br Conewago Creek | 1-84' | | Burr | |
| SW of Irishtown | | T | S Br Conewago Creek | 1-93' | 1881 | Burr | Joseph J. Smith |
| SW of New Oxford | Kohler's Mill | | S Br Conewago Creek | 1-90' | | Burr | |
| SW of York Springs | Heike's | | Bermudian Creek | 1-64' | | Burr | |
| SW of York Springs | Spangler's | | Bermudian Creek | 1-89' | | Burr | |
| N of Brush Run | | T | Swift Run | 1-73' | 1863 | Burr | |
| SW of Gettysburg | Sauk's | T | Marsh Creek | 1-91' | 1854 | Town | |
| S of Bermudian | | T | Muddy Run | 1-70' | | Burr | |
| SW of Fairfield | Jack's Mountain | T | Toms Creek | 1-64' | 1862 | Burr | |

## PENNSYLVANIA

| LOCATION | NAME | OWN-ER | STREAM | SPANS & LENGTH | DATE | TYPE | BUILDER, ETC. |
|---|---|---|---|---|---|---|---|
| **BEDFORD COUNTY** | | | | | | | |
| E of Keeg | | T | Raystown Br, Juniata River | 1-88' | 1892 | Burr | |
| W of Mann's Choice | Diehl's | | Raystown Br, Juniata River | 1-88' | 1892 | Burr | [5] |
| N of Mann's Choice | Kinton | T | Raystown Br, Juniata River | 1-130' | 1902 | Burr | Wilson H. Williams |
| N of New Paris | | | Dunning Creek | 1-60' | | Burr | J.H. Thompson[6] |
| E of Ryot | | | Dunning Creek | 1-76' | | Burr | |
| SE of Pleasantville | | P | Dunning Creek | 1-81' | | Burr | Bypassed |
| SE of Pleasantville | | | Dunning Creek | 1-69' | | Burr | |
| S of Reynoldsdale | | T | Dunning Creek | 1-120' | 1880 | Burr | |
| N of Bedford | Hughes Station | T | Dunning Creek | 1-90' | 1878 | Burr | J.H. Thompson |
| N of Bedford | Yount | T | Dunning Creek | 1-123' | 1875 | Burr | |
| Gapsville | | T | Brush Creek | 1-65' | 1891 | Burr | W.H. Williams |
| SW of Breezewood | | | Brush Run | 1-78' | [7] | Burr | |
| E of Mench | Felton's Mill | T | Brush Creek | 1-100' | 1892 | Burr | W.S. Mullin |
| W of Breezewood | Jackson's Mills | | Brush Run | 1-121' | 1902 | Burr | |
| W of Breezewood | McDaniels | | Brush Run | 1-96' | 1871 | Burr | Jacob Fries |
| SE of Clearville | | T | Shaffer's Creek | 1-74' | 1882 | Q-P | |
| N of Mattie | | T | Shaffer's Creek | 1-90' | 1891 | Burr | |
| W of Palo Alto | | | Gladdens Run | 1-60' | 1880 | Q-P | Harmon Walters |

[1]Originally over Monocacy River; rebuilt here after '89 flood.    [2]SE of Arendtsville.    [3]Or Peepytown.    [4]And David Zeigler, Jr.    [5]A. K. Battenfield and Sons.    [6]By-passed.    [7]1875 or 1889 (?).

| LOCATION | NAME | OWN-ER | STREAM | SPANS & LENGTH | DATE | TYPE | BUILDER, ETC. |
|---|---|---|---|---|---|---|---|
| S of Palo Alto | Cook's Mill | T | Gladdens Run | 1–54' | 1881 | Q-P | Harmon Walters |
| W of Osterburg | | | Bob's Creek | 1–81' | | Burr | |
| SE of Bedford Valley | Cruse | | Br of Evitt's Creek | 1–66' | | Burr | |
| NW of Robinsonville | | T | Br of Sideline Hill Creek | 1–70' | 1881 | Burr | |
| E of Ott Town | | T | Cove Creek | 1–64' | 1887 | Burr | |
| S of Schellsburg | | | Shawnee Branch | 1–66' | | MK-P | |
| Chaneysville | | T | Sweet Root Creek | 1–60' | 1892 | Burr | |
| E of Hewitt | | | Town Creek | 1–72' | | Burr | |
| E of Yellow Creek | Halls Mill | | Yellow Creek | 1–80' | 1874 | Burr | |

## BERKS COUNTY

| LOCATION | NAME | OWN-ER | STREAM | SPANS & LENGTH | DATE | TYPE | BUILDER, ETC. |
|---|---|---|---|---|---|---|---|
| SE of Bernville | Conrad's | | Tulpehocken Creek | 1–145' | 1839 | Burr | |
| NW of Reading | Van Reed Paper Mill | T | Tulpehocken Creek | 1–144' | 1837 | Burr | |
| NW of Reading | Red (or Wertz) | | Tulpehocken Creek | 1–204' | 1867 | Burr | clear span 198'8 |
| Spangsville | Griesemer's Mill | | Manatawny Creek | 1–124' | 1832 | Burr | |
| S of Pleasantville | Pleasantville | T | Little Manatawny Creek | 1–126' | 1852 | Burr | R'dway over arches |
| Dreibelbis | Dreibelbis | | Maiden Creek | 1–172' | 1869 | Burr | |
| MN of Kutztown | Kutz Mill (or Sacony) | | Sacony Creek | 1–93' | 1854 | Burr | Bitner & Ahrens |

## BLAIR COUNTY

| LOCATION | NAME | OWN-ER | STREAM | SPANS & LENGTH | DATE | TYPE | BUILDER, ETC. |
|---|---|---|---|---|---|---|---|
| SE of Tyrone | Fuoss Mill | | Little Juniata River | 1–126' | 1874 | Burr | Jacob Fries |

## BRADFORD COUNTY

| LOCATION | NAME | OWN-ER | STREAM | SPANS & LENGTH | DATE | TYPE | BUILDER, ETC. |
|---|---|---|---|---|---|---|---|
| E of Burlington | Luther's Mills | | Brown's Creek | 1–77' | 1857 | Burr | 9 |

## BUCKS COUNTY

| LOCATION | NAME | OWN-ER | STREAM | SPANS & LENGTH | DATE | TYPE | BUILDER, ETC. |
|---|---|---|---|---|---|---|---|
| E of Pipersville | Loux's | T | Cabin Run | 1–81' | 1874 | Town | David Sutton |
| E of Pt. Pleasant | Cabin Run | | Cabin Run | 1–56' | 1871 | Town | |
| W of Durham | Houpt's (Witte's) Mill | | Cook's or Durham Creek | 1–90' | 1872 | Town | |
| Erwinna | | T | Swamp or Lodi Creek | 1–40' | | Town | |
| N of Pt. Pleasant | Frankenfield's | | Tinicum Creek | 1–110' | 1872 | Town | David Sutton |
| E of Perkasie | Mood's (or Branch) | T | NE Br of Perkiomen Creek | 1–100' | 1874 | Town | |
| N of New Britain | Pine Valley | | Pine Run | 1–81' | 10 | Town | David Sutton |
| E of Quakertown | Sheard's (or Thatcher) | T | Tohickon Creek | 1–114' | 1876 | Town | |
| E of Pleasant Valley | Sleifer's (or Knecht's) | | Cook Creek | 1–90' | 1873 | Town | |
| Uhlertown | Lock #8 | | 11 | 1–85' | | Town | |
| S of New Hope | Van Sandt's | | Pidcock Creek | 1–70' | 1873 | Town | G. Arnst12 |
| NW of Newtown | Twining Ford | P | Neshaminy Creek | 2–155' | | Town | |
| Perkasie | South Perkasie | | over dry land | 1–85' | 1832 | Town | Moved Lenape Pk, '58 |

## CARBON COUNTY

| LOCATION | NAME | OWN-ER | STREAM | SPANS & LENGTH | DATE | TYPE | BUILDER, ETC. |
|---|---|---|---|---|---|---|---|
| E of Harrity | | | Big or Pohopoco Creek | 1–82' | | MK-P | |
| Little Gap | | | Princess Creek | 1–87' | | Burr | |

## CHESTER COUNTY

| LOCATION | NAME | OWN-ER | STREAM | SPANS & LENGTH | DATE | TYPE | BUILDER, ETC. |
|---|---|---|---|---|---|---|---|
| Mortonville | | P | W Br Brandywine Creek | 1–99' | 1876 | Burr | Menander Wood |
| E of Embreeville | Glen Hall | | W Br Brandywine Creek | 2–168' | 1881 | Burr | Menander Wood13 |
| S of Downingtown | Gibson's | | E Br Brandywine Creek | 1–78' | 1872 | Burr | ThomasDoan |
| Sheeder | Halls | T | French Creek | 1–100' | 1850 | Burr | Robert Russell14 |
| N of Kimberton | Kennedy's | | French Creek | 1–115' | 1856 | Burr | A. Kennedy & J. King |
| W of Phoenixville | Rapp's | | French Creek | 1–122' | 1866 | Burr | Benjamin F. Hartman |
| NE of Hickory Hill | Linton Stevens | | Big Elk Creek | 1–105' | 1886 | Burr | |
| N of Lewisville | Rudolph & Arthur's | | Big Elk Creek | 1–80' | 1880 | Burr | Menander Wood |
| W of Lewisville | Glen Hope | | Little Elk Creek | 1–65' | 1889 | Burr | Menander Wood |
| N of Doe Run | Speakman's No. 115 | T | Buck Run | 1–74' | 1881 | Burr | |
| NE of Doe Run | Speakman's No. 2 (TB) | | Buck Run | 1–76' | 1902 | Burr | |
| NE of Doe Run | Hayes Clark (TB) | | Doe Run | 1–78' | 1884 | Burr | Menander Wood |
| N of Fremont | McCreary's | | Black Run | 1–87' | 1889 | Burr | George E. Jones |
| SE of Milford Mills | Larkins | | Marsh Creek | 1–69' | 1881 | Burr | M. & F. Wood |
| Valley Forge Park | Knox's | T | Valley Creek | 1–50' | 1865 | Burr | Robert Russell |
| E of Landenburg | Yeatman's | T | E Br White Clay Creek | 1–75' | 1874 | Burr | Peter Burns, Jr. |

## CHESTER-DELAWARE COUNTIES

| LOCATION | NAME | OWN-ER | STREAM | SPANS & LENGTH | DATE | TYPE | BUILDER, ETC. |
|---|---|---|---|---|---|---|---|
| W of Newtown Square | Bartram's | | Crum Creek | 1–60' | 1860 | Burr | F. Wood (unused) |

## CHESTER-LANCASTER COUNTIES

| LOCATION | NAME | OWN-ER | STREAM | SPANS & LENGTH | DATE | TYPE | BUILDER, ETC. |
|---|---|---|---|---|---|---|---|
| S of Atglen | Mercer's Ford | | Octoraro Creek | 1–103' | 1880 | Burr | B. J. Carter |
| W of Homeville | Newcomer's | | Octoraro Creek | 1–98' | 1888 | Burr | |
| Bellbank | Bellbank | T | Octoraro Creek | 1–131' | 1861 | Burr | Robert Russell |
| W of Oxford | Pine Grove | | Octoraro Creek | 2–204' | 1884 | Burr | Elias McMellen |

## CLEARFIELD COUNTY

| LOCATION | NAME | OWN-ER | STREAM | SPANS & LENGTH | DATE | TYPE | BUILDER, ETC. |
|---|---|---|---|---|---|---|---|
| McGee's Mills | | | W Br Susquehanna River | 1–109' | | Burr | |

---

8Longest in Pennsylvania.    101842 or 1874 (?).    12And P. S. Naylor.    14And Jacob Fox.

9Highest covered bridge above water    11Delaware Valley division of    13And Richard Pearson.    15Or M. A. Pyle.

in Pennsylvania.    Pennsylvania Canal.

| Location | Name | Owner | Stream | Spans & Length | Date | Type | Builder, etc. |
|---|---|---|---|---|---|---|---|
| **CLINTON COUNTY** | | | | | | | |
| near Tylersville | Logan Mills | T | Big Fishing Creek | 1–59′ | 1874 | Q–P | |
| **COLUMBIA COUNTY** | | | | | | | |
| SE of Central | "Y" | | E Br Fishing Creek | 1–76′ | | Q–P | |
| Laubach | Welle Hess | T | Fishing Creek | 1–114′ | | Burr | |
| Stillwater | Stillwater | | Fishing Creek | 1–151′ | 1849 | Burr | preserved[16] |
| Rupert | Rupert | | Fishing Creek | 1–185½′ | | Burr | |
| SW of Waller | Creasyville | | Little Fishing Creek | 1–45′ | | Q–P | |
| SW of Waller | Jud Christian | | Little Fishing Creek | 1–56′ | | Q–P | |
| NE of Sereno | Cole's | T | Little Fishing Creek | 1–59′ | | Q–P | |
| NE of Sereno | Sam Eckman's | | Little Fishing Creek | 1–66′ | | Q–P | |
| NE of Sereno | Greenley | T | Little Fishing Creek | 1–69′ | | Q–P | |
| S of Millville | Beyers | | Little Fishing Creek | 1–77′ | | Ar. Q–P | |
| Mordansville Sta. | Mordansville | T | Little Fishing Creek | 1–119′ | | Burr | |
| SE of Mordsv. Sta. | Stauffer's | | Little Fishing Creek | 1–118′ | | Burr | |
| N of Buckhorn Sta. | Wanich | | Little Fishing Creek | 1–99′ | | Burr | |
| W of Buckhorn Sta. | Muesteller[17] | T | Little Fishing Creek | 1–121′ | c1860 | Burr | |
| NW of Mill Grove | Wagner | | Roaring Creek | 1–54′ | | Q–P | |
| W of Mill Grove | Snyder | | Roaring Creek | 1–60′ | | Q–P | |
| E of Slabtown | Yeager | | Roaring Creek | 1–55′ | | Q–P | unused |
| W of Slabtown | Davis | | Roaring Creek | 1–87′ | | Burr | |
| E of Pensyl's Mill | Esther Furnace | | Roaring Creek | 2–103′ | | Q–P | |
| E of Pensyl's Mill | Parrs Mill | | Roaring Creek | 1–83′ | | Burr | |
| NW of Pensyl's Mill | Riegel | | Roaring Creek | 1–107′ | | Burr | |
| N of Knoebel's Grove | Rhorbach | | S Br Roaring Creek | 1–66′ | | Q–P | |
| N of Knoebel's Grove | Reeder | | S Br Roaring Creek | 1–112′ | 1885 | Burr | John Eves |
| Jonestown | | T | Huntington Creek | 1–108′ | | Burr | |
| W of Jonestown | Josiah Hess | T | Huntington Creek | 1–105′ | | Burr | |
| E of Forks | East Paden (TB) | T | Huntington Creek | 1–72′ | | Q–P | |
| E of Forks | West Paden (TB) | T | Huntington Creek | 1–92′ | | Burr | |
| Mainville | | | Catawissa Creek | 1–105′ | | Burr | |
| NE of Catawissa | Hollingshead | | Catawissa Creek | 1–114′ | | Burr | |
| N of Orangeville | Kline | T | Green Creek | 1–71′ | | Q–P | |
| N of Orangeville | Patterson | | Green Creek | 1–82′ | | Burr | |
| N of Iola | Shoemaker's | T | Branch Run | 1–52′ | | Q–P | |
| SW of Rohrsburg | Kramer | | Mud Run | 1–50′ | | Q–P | |
| E of Knoebel's Grove | Johnson | | Musser or Mugser Run | 1–61′ | | Q–P | |
| Fowlersville | | T | Briar Creek | 1–40′ | | Q–P | |
| NE of Jonestown | Buckalew | | Pine Creek | 1–63′ | | Q–P | |
| E of Benton | Joe Ash | T | Raven Creek | 1–37′ | | Q–P | |
| **COLUMBIA-MONTOUR COUNTIES** | | | | | | | |
| Roaring Creek[18] | | T | Roaring Creek | 1–74′ | | Burr | |
| **COLUMBIA-NORTHUMBERLAND COUNTIES** | | | | | | | |
| N of Bear Gap | Krickbaum's | | S Br Roaring Creek | 1–61′ | | Q–P | Built on a skew |
| S of Knoebel's Grove | Richard's | | S Br Roaring Creek | 1–68′ | | MK–P | Built 1875 |
| Knoebel's Grove | | | S Br Roaring Creek | 1–38′ | 1935 | Q–P | [19] |
| **CUMBERLAND COUNTY** | | | | | | | |
| E of Newburg | Ramp's | | Conodoguinet Creek | 1–136′ | 1882 | Burr | |
| W of Newville | Thompson's | | Conodoguinet Creek | 1–149′ | 1853 | Burr | |
| NE of Newville | Graham | | Conodoguinet Creek | 1–195′ | 1857 | Burr | |
| Keiter's Mill | Stanton | | Conodoguinet Creek | 1–160′ | 1855 | Burr | |
| Greider's Mill | Greider's | T | Conodoguinet Creek | 2–222′ | 1851 | Burr | |
| NE of Plainfield | Burgner | | Conodoguinet Creek | 2–234′ | 1889 | Burr | |
| W of Carlisle | Hays | | Conodoguinet Creek | 1–110′ | 1825 | Burr | John & Joseph Hays[20] |
| NW of Carlisle | Watts | T | Conodoguinet Creek | 2–208′ | 1889 | Burr | |
| NW of Carlisle | Waggoner's | T | Conodoguinet Creek | 2–206′ | 1889 | Burr | |
| NE of Middlesex | Bernheisel | | Conodoguinet Creek | 2–195′ | 1869 | Burr | |
| N of New Kingston | Silv. Spr. (or Old Iron) | T | Conodoguinet Creek | 2–246′ | 1884 | Burr | Portal ends differ |
| Sporting Hill | Erb | T | Conodoguinet Creek | 2–318′ | 1893 | Burr | |
| **CUMBERLAND-YORK COUNTIES** | | | | | | | |
| Bowmansdale | | T | Yellow Breeches Creek | 1–127′ | 1867 | Burr | |
| S of Lemoyne | Spangler's | T | Yellow Breeches Creek | 1–134′ | 1850 | Burr | |
| **DAUPHIN COUNTY** | | | | | | | |
| Sand Beach | Sand Beach | T | Swatara Creek | 2–220′ | | Burr | |
| Hummelstown | Fiddler's Elbow | | Swatara Creek | 2–205′ | | Burr | |
| N of Middletown | Clifton | T | Swatara Creek | 2–234′ | | Burr | |

[16]Daniel and James McHenry, builders, and John H. Edson, foreman.

[17]Or Van Der Slice.

[18]West of Catawissa.

[19]Built near Benton, moved here in '35.

[20]Oldest known existing covered bridge in U.S.

| Location | Name | Own-er | Stream | Spans & Length | Date | Type | Builders, etc. |
|---|---|---|---|---|---|---|---|
| Oakdale Station | Picnic grounds | | Wisconisco Creek | 1–58' | | Burr[21] | |
| NW of Loyalton | Stroup | | Wisconisco Creek | 1–61½' | | Burr | |
| NW of Elizabethville | Cooper Farm | | Wisconisco Creek | 1–77' | | Burr | |
| NW of Elizabethville | Mattas Mill | | Wisconisco Creek | 1–75' | | Burr | |
| NW of Elizabethville | | T | Wisconisco Creek | 1–73' | | Burr | |
| S of Berrysburg | | T | Wisconisco Creek | 1–68' | | Burr | |
| Woodside Station | | | Wisconisco Creek | 1–84' | | Burr | |

## DAUPHIN-LANCASTER COUNTIES

| | | | | | | | |
|---|---|---|---|---|---|---|---|
| NE of Falmouth | Nissley's Mill | | Conewago Creek | 1–81' | 1852 | Burr | Messner & Linker |

## DAUPHIN-NORTHUMBERLAND COUNTIES

| | | | | | | | |
|---|---|---|---|---|---|---|---|
| W of Hebe | Troutman's | | Mahantango Creek | 1–110' | | Burr | |
| Pillow | | T | Mahantango Creek | 1–103' | | Burr | |
| W of County Line | Deibler's Mill | | Mahantango Creek | 1–104' | | Burr | |

## DELAWARE COUNTY

| | | | | | | | |
|---|---|---|---|---|---|---|---|
| W of Manoa | Smith's Sawmill | P | Sawmill Creek | 1–16½' | 1952 | Q-P | Robert H. Smith |

## ERIE COUNTY

| | | | | | | | |
|---|---|---|---|---|---|---|---|
| Keepville | | T | Conneaut Creek | 1–78' | 1897 | MK-P | W. Sherman |
| E of Cherry Hill | Perry | | Conneaut Creek | 1– | | MK-P | W. Sherman |
| W. of Keepville | Sherman | T | W Br Conneaut Creek | 1–72' | | MK-P | W. Sherman |
| SE of Girard | Gudgeonville | | Elk Creek | 1–72' | | MK-P | W. Sherman |
| SE of Waterford | | | LeBoeuf Creek | 1–75' | | Town | |

## FRANKLIN COUNTY

| | | | | | | | |
|---|---|---|---|---|---|---|---|
| Upton–Milnor | Martin's Mill | | Conococheague Creek | 2–205' | | Town | |
| near Welsh Run | Witherspoon's (or Red) | | Licking Creek | 1–87' | | Burr | Samuel Stouffer |

## GREENE COUNTY

| | | | | | | | |
|---|---|---|---|---|---|---|---|
| W of Whiteley | White | | Whiteley Creek | 1–67' | 1900 | Q-P | |
| W of Garard's Fort | Neil's (or Red) | | Whiteley Creek | 1–86' | 1900 | Burr | |
| E. of Garard's Fort | Willow Tree | | Whiteley Creek | 2–94' | 1875 | Q-P | |
| S of Carmichael's | Paisley | T | Little Whiteley Creek | 1–39' | 1880 | Q-P | |
| W of Brave | Dunkard | T | Thoms Run | 1–55' | | Q-P | |
| Pine Bank | | T | Thoms Run | 1–29' | 1870 | K-P | |
| N of McCracken | Smith | T | Dunkard Fk of Wheeling Creek | 1–55' | 1880 | Q-P | |
| NW of Durbin | Keyes | T | Dunkard Fk of Wheeling Creek | 1–94' | | Burr | |
| SW of Bristoria | Hughes | T | N Fk of Wheeling Creek | 1–50' | c1870 | Q-P | |
| E of Ruff Creek | | | Ruff Creek | 1–30' | 1900 | K-P | |
| NW of Mather | Lippincott | | Ruff Creek | 1–27' | 1943 | K-P | Benjamin F. Lewellen |
| Jollytown | | T | Garrison Fk of Dunkard Creek | 1–45' | 1880 | Q-P | |
| E of Fairchance | Barker Ford | | Dunkard Creek | 1–127' | 1878 | Burr | |
| E of Rutan | Scott | | S Fk of Ten Mile Creek | 1–41' | 1885 | Q-P | William Lang |
| S of Ryerson | Bryan | | Barney's Run | 1–77' | 1900 | Burr | Steven Acklin |
| SE of Deep Valley | | T | Bissett Run | 1–49' | 1907 | Q-P | Edward Mankey |
| Pine Bank | | T | Blockhouse Run | 1–40' | 1870 | Q-P | Unhoused, 1957 |
| S of McCracken | Sugar Grove | T | Chambers Run | 1–39' | 1910 | Q-P | |
| W of Deep Valley | | T | Coon Run | 1–34' | 1910 | Q-P | Edward Mankey |
| S of Fordyce | | T | Frosty Run | 1–37' | 1885 | Q-P | |
| SW of Jollytown | Hero | T | Hagan Creek[22] | 1–39' | 1887 | Q-P | T. M. Hennen |
| S of Rogersville | Shriver | | Hargus Creek | 1–39' | 1900 | Q-P | |
| W of Mt Morris | Pethel | T | Rudolph Run | 1–41' | 1882 | Q-P | |
| S of Waynesburg | White Barn | T | Smith Creek | 1–29' | 1888 | Q-P | |
| S of Kuhntown | King | | Hoover Run | 1–50' | | Q-P | |
| SW of Bristoria | | T | Long Run | 1–30' | c1897 | K-P | Walter Teagarden |
| Carmichaels | | | Muddy Creek | 1–54' | 1889 | Q-P | |
| Waynesburg | Red Bird Hollow | | Purman Run | 1–30' | 1900 | K-P | |
| N of Oak Forest | Neddie Woods | | Pursley Creek | 1–40' | 1900 | Q-P | |

## GREENE-WASHINGTON COUNTIES

| | | | | | | | |
|---|---|---|---|---|---|---|---|
| E of Zollarsville | Hawkins | | Ten Mile Creek | 1–111' | 1900 | Burr | |
| E of Zollarsville | Davis[23] | | Ten Mile Creek | 1–96' | 1900 | Burr | |

## HUNTINGDON COUNTY

| | | | | | | | |
|---|---|---|---|---|---|---|---|
| N of Shade Gap | | | Shade Creek | 1–57' | 1889 | Howe | |

## INDIANA COUNTY

| | | | | | | | |
|---|---|---|---|---|---|---|---|
| Nashville | | T | Little Mahoning Creek | 1–80' | 1882 | Town | |
| SE of Smicksburg | | T | Little Mahoning Creek | 1–105' | 1881 | Town | |
| SW of Davis | | | S Br Plum Creek | 1–39' | | Town | |
| SW of Davis | | | S Br Plum Creek | 1–39' | | Town | |
| SE of Home | Kintersburg | | Crooked Creek | 1–66' | | Howe | |
| near Thomas | | | Crooked Creek | 1–88' | | Town | |

[21]And Queenpost.     [22]Or Penna. fork of Dunkard Creek.     [23]Or Oberholtzer or Horne.

| Location | Name | Owner | Stream | Spans & Length | Date | Type | Builder, etc. |
|---|---|---|---|---|---|---|---|
| **JUNIATA COUNTY** | | | | | | | |
| E of McCoysville | McCoy | T | Tuscarora Creek | 1–112' | | Burr | |
| Academia | Pomeroy | T | Tuscarora Creek | 2–261' | 1901 | Burr | James Goniger |
| W of Seven Stars | Dimmsville | T | Cocolamus Creek | 1–100' | | Burr | |
| Port Royal | | T | Licking Creek | 2–98' | | Burr | |
| **JUNIATA-SNYDER COUNTIES** | | | | | | | |
| N of Oriental | | T | Mahantango Creek | 1–57' | | MK–P[24] | |
| E of Oriental | | T | Mahantango Creek | 1–88' | 1907 | Burr | |
| **LANCASTER COUNTY** | | | | | | | |
| W of Churchtown | Pool Forge | T | Conestoga Creek | 1–99' | 1859 | Burr | Levi Fink |
| N of Goodville | Isaac Shearer's Mill | | Conestoga Creek | 1–88' | 1878 | Burr | B. C. Carter |
| SW of Martindale | Bear's Mill | | Conestoga Creek | 1–94' | 1876 | Burr | W. W. Upp |
| S of Murrell | Martins Mill | T | Conestoga Creek | 1–98' | 1846 | Burr | George Fink[25] |
| near Oregon | Nolt's Point Mill | | Conestoga Creek | 1–133' | 1867 | Burr | Elias McMellen |
| Hunsecker | Hunsecker's Mill | T | Conestoga Creek | 1–180' | 1848 | Burr | Joseph Russell |
| Eden | Groff's Factory | T | Conestoga Creek | 1–158' | 1848 | Burr | Israel Groff |
| S of Lancaster | Snavely's Mill[26] | | Conestoga Creek | 2–349' | 1850 | Burr | Benjamin Snavely |
| E of Millersville | Wabank | T | Conestoga Creek | 2–246' | 1841 | Burr | Jacob Huber |
| Oreville | Landis Mill | | Little Conestoga Creek | 1–53' | 1873 | MK–P | |
| NW of Bausman | Stoneroad's Mill | P | Little Conestoga Creek | 1–55' | 1868 | K–P | Elias McMellen |
| NE of Leaman Place | | | Pequea Creek | 1–113' | 1893 | Burr | |
| SW of Soudersburg | Herr's Mill | | Pequea Creek | 2–178' | 1844 | Burr | |
| W of Strasburg | Neff's Mill | | Pequea Creek | 1–102' | 1875 | Burr | |
| Lime Valley | Hurtzinger's Mill | | Pequea Creek | 1–104' | 1871 | Burr | |
| NE of Marticville | Good's Fording | T | Pequea Creek | 1–79' | 1855 | Burr | |
| NE of Marticville | Baumgardner's Mill | | Pequea Creek | 1–111' | 1860 | Burr | |
| Colemanville | | | Pequea Creek | 1–170' | 1856 | Burr | |
| NE of Sporting Hill | Kaufman's Distillery | | Chickies Creek | 1–96' | 1874 | Burr | |
| S of Lancaster Junction | Shearer's | | Chickies Creek | 1–40' | 1856 | Burr | |
| N of Salunga | Shenk's Mill | | Chickies Creek | 1–96' | 1855 | Burr | |
| NW of Silver Spring | Moore's Mill | | Chickies Creek | 1–80' | 1885 | Burr | |
| W of Silver Spring | Forry's | | Chickies Creek | 1–103' | 1869 | Burr | |
| SW of New Town | Amwake's Mill | T | Chickies Creek | 1–133' | 1875 | Burr | |
| N of Mt. Joy | Risser's Mill | T | Arm of Little Chickies Creek | 1–68' | 1849 | Burr | |
| E of Marietta | Johnson's Mill | | Little Chickies Creek | 1–80' | 1867 | Burr | Elias McMellen |
| Reamstown | Bucher's Mill | | Cocalico Creek | 1–60' | 1891 | Burr | Elias McMellen |
| Akron | Keller's Mill | | Cocalico Creek | 1–76' | 1891 | Burr | Elias McMellen |
| W of Brownstown | Rose Hill | | Cocalico Creek | 1–89' | 1849 | Burr | Henry Zook |
| W of Bartville | Jackson's Mill | | W Br Octoraro Creek | 1–156' | 1878 | Burr | |
| Kings Bridge | | T | W Br Octoraro Creek | 1–72' | 1884 | Burr | |
| White Rock | White Rock Forge | | W Br Octoraro Creek | 1–87' | 1847 | Burr | |
| NW of Terre Hill | Oberholtzer's Mill | T | Muddy Creek | 1–128' | 1866 | Burr | |
| E of Hahnstown | Fry's Mill | | Muddy Creek | 1–95' | 1849 | Burr | |
| W of Refton | Miller's Mill | T | Big Beaver Creek | 1–75' | 1871 | Burr | Elias McMellen |
| NW of Millway | Samuel Erb's | | Hammer Creek | 1–80' | 1887 | Burr | |
| N of Millway | Hess Mill | T | Middle Creek | 1–58' | 1844 | Burr | |
| **LAWRENCE COUNTY** | | | | | | | |
| S of Rose Point | McConnell's Mills | | Slippery Rock Creek | 1–93' | 1874 | Howe | |
| N of Neshannock Falls | Banks | | Neshannock Creek | 1–117' | 1888 | Burr | |
| **LEHIGH COUNTY** | | | | | | | |
| W of Schnecksville | Schlicher's | T | Jordan Creek | 1–100' | 1882 | Burr | |
| S of Schnecksville | Rex's | | Jordan Creek | 1–111' | 1858 | Burr | |
| S of Schnecksville | Geiger's | | Jordan Creek | 1–105' | 1858 | Burr | |
| E of Siegersville | Manassas Guth | | Jordan Creek | 1–107' | 1858 | Burr | |
| E of Siegersville | Wehr's or Sieger's | | Jordan Creek | 1–111' | 1841 | Burr | |
| SE of Allentown | Bogert's | T | Little Lehigh River | 1–145' | 1841 | Burr | Preserved |
| **LUZERNE COUNTY** | | | | | | | |
| nr. Huntington Mills | | P | Huntington Creek | 1–54' | | Q–P | |
| **LYCOMING COUNTY** | | | | | | | |
| SW of Lairdsville | | | Little Muncy Creek | 1–98' | 1888 | Burr | |
| SW of Cogan House | Buckhorn | | Larrys Creek | 1–92' | 1877 | Burr | |
| N of Buttonwood | | | Blockhouse Creek | 1–69' | 1898 | MK–P | |
| **MERCER COUNTY** | | | | | | | |
| S of Shenango | Kidd's Mill | | Shenango River | 1–110' | | Smith | |
| **MONROE COUNTY** | | | | | | | |
| Swiftwater | Swiftwater Inn | | Swiftwater Creek | 1–36' | 1956 | K–P | |

[24]And Queenpost.          [25]And Samuel Reamsnyder.          [26]Or Second Lock.

| Location | Name | Owner | Stream | Spans & Length | Date | Type | Builder, etc. |
|---|---|---|---|---|---|---|---|
| **MONTOUR-NORTHUMBERLAND COUNTIES** | | | | | | | |
| NE of Potts Grove | | | Chillisquaque Creek | 1–86′ | | Burr | |
| **NORTHAMPTON COUNTY** | | | | | | | |
| N of Northampton | Solt's Mill | T | Hockendauqua Creek | 1–96′ | 1840 | Burr | |
| **NORTHUMBERLAND COUNTY** | | | | | | | |
| E of Hunter | | | Mahanoy Creek | 1–105′ | 1842 | Burr | |
| N of Herndon | Bohmen Mill | | Mahanoy Creek | 1–90′ | | Burr | |
| Keefer Sta. | | | Shamokin Creek | 1–110′ | | Burr | |
| NE of Chillisquaque | | | Chillisquaque Creek | 1– | | Burr | |
| N of Dewart | | | Delaware Run | 1–98′ | | MK–P | |
| Rebuck | | | Schwaben Creek | 1–31′ | | K–P | |
| **PERRY COUNTY** | | | | | | | |
| New Germantown | | | Shermans Creek | 1–61′ | | MK–P[27] | |
| S of Mt. Pleasant | | | Shermans Creek | 1–61′ | | Q–P | |
| W of Blain | | | Shermans Creek | 1–76′ | | Burr | |
| S of Andersonburg | Flickinger's Mill | T | Shermans Creek | 1–98′ | | Burr | |
| E of Andersonburg | | T | Shermans Creek | 2–144′ | | Burr | |
| SW of Loysville | | T | Shermans Creek | 2–145′ | | Burr | |
| S of Loysville | Weavers Mill | T | Shermans Creek | 2–117′ | | Burr | Two Auxil. Piers[28] |
| S of Landisburg | Reist's | | Shermans Creek | 1– | | Burr[29] | Auxil. Pier |
| Dellville | | | Shermans Creek | 2–183′ | | Burr | |
| Saville | | T | Big Buffalo Creek | 1–60′ | | Burr | |
| S of Saville | | | Big Buffalo Creek | 1–61′ | | Q–P | |
| NW of Newport | | | Big Buffalo Creek | 1–113′ | | Burr | |
| N of Bloomfield | Wahneta | | Little Buffalo Creek | 1–74′ | | Burr | |
| Loysville[30] | Wagner's[31] | | Bixler's Run | 1–74′ | | Burr | |
| S of Blain | Manassa | T | Bull or Houston's Run | 1–50′ | | Burr | |
| W of Liverpool | | T | Wildcat Creek | 1–45′ | | MK–P[32] | |
| **PHILADELPHIA COUNTY** | | | | | | | |
| Fairmount Park | Thomas Mill | | Wissahickon Creek | 1–78′ | | Howe | |
| **SCHUYLKILL COUNTY** | | | | | | | |
| Dow | | | Bear Creek | 1–39′ | | Burr | |
| Rock | | | Bear Creek | 1–43′ | | Burr | |
| **SNYDER COUNTY** | | | | | | | |
| NE of Lowell | | T | Middle Creek | 1–32′ | | Q–P | |
| NW of Beaver Springs | | | Middle Creek | 1–90′ | | Burr | |
| N of Beavertown | | | Middle Creek | 1–87′ | | Burr | |
| N of Meiserville | | | N Br Mahantango Creek | 1–54′ | | Burr | |
| **SOMERSET COUNTY** | | | | | | | |
| NW of New Lexington | Barronvale | T | Laurel Hill Creek | 2–139′ | | Burr | |
| W of New Lexington | Kings | | Laurel Hill Creek | 1–120′ | 1906 | Burr | Preserved |
| Humbert | Upper Humbert | | Laurel Hill Creek | 1–84′ | | Burr | |
| N of Ursina | Lower Humbert | | Laurel Hill Creek | 1–90′ | 1891 | Burr | |
| N of Fairhope | | | Brush Creek | 1–59′ | 1870 | K–P | |
| NW of Fairhope | Packsaddle | T | Brush Creek | 1–59′ | 1870 | MK–P | |
| Shanksville | | | Stony Creek | 1–81′ | | Burr | |
| NW of Shanksville | | | Stony Creek | 1–110′ | c1880 | MK–P | |
| S of Stoystown | Kantner | | Stony Creek | 1–84′ | | K–P[33] | Closed |
| NW of Tire Hill | | | Bens Creek | 1–48′ | | Burr | |
| NE of Garrett | Beechdale | | Buffalo Creek | 1–42′ | 1870 | Burr | |
| Roberts | | | Coxe's Creek | 1–52′ | | Burr | |
| New Baltimore | | | Raystown Br Juniata River | 1–69′ | | Q–P | |
| **SULLIVAN COUNTY** | | | | | | | |
| Forksville | | T | Loyalsock Creek | 1–156′ | 1850 | Burr | Salder Rogers |
| NE of Hillsgrove | | | Loyalsock Creek | 1–171′ | | Burr | |
| S of Sonestown | | | Muncy Creek | 1–99′ | | Burr | |
| **UNION COUNTY** | | | | | | | |
| W of Mifflinburg | | | Buffalo Creek | 1–70′ | | MK–P[34] | |
| Mifflinburg | Fourth Street | | Buffalo Creek | 1–80′ | | Burr | |
| NW of Lewisburg | | | Little Buffalo Creek | 1–30′ | | K–P | At penitentiary |
| W of Millmont | Red | | Penn Creek | 1–151′ | 1855 | Burr | |
| W of White Deer | | | White Deer Creek | 1–57′ | | Q–P | |
| **WASHINGTON COUNTY** | | | | | | | |
| S of Prosperity | Day | | Upper Ten Mile Creek | 1–32′ | c1875 | Q–P | |
| W of Marianna | Bailey | | Ten Mile Creek | 1–66′ | 1889 | Burr | |

[27]And Queenpost.  [29]And two Queenpost.  [31]Or Thompson's.  [33]And Queenpost.

[28]And two types of Burr trusses.  [30]West of Fort Robinson.  [32]And Queenpost.  [34]And Kingpost.

| Location | Name | Owner | Stream | Spans & Length | Date | Type | Builder, etc. |
|---|---|---|---|---|---|---|---|
| W of Ten Mile | Hughes | | Ten Mile Creek | 1–66' | 1889 | Q–P | |
| W of Marianna | Martins Mill[35] | | Ten Mile Creek | 1–50' | 1889 | Q–P | |
| W of East Finley | Sprowls | | Rocky Run | 1–27' | | K–P | |
| East Finley | Montgomery | T | Rocky Run | 1–29' | 1875 | K–P | Unhoused 1958 |
| N of West Finley | Danley | T | Robinson Run | 1–50' | | Q–P | |
| NW of West Finley | Wyit Sprowls | | Robinson Run | 1–43' | | Q–P | |
| N of W Finley | McCoy | | Robinson Run | 1–50' | | Q–P | |
| N of W Finley | Crawford | | Robinson Run | 1–54' | | Q–P | |
| W of E Finley | Brownlee | | [36] | 1–31' | | K–P | |
| East Finley | Plants | | [36] | 1–24' | | K–P | |
| SE of W Finley | Longdon | | [36] | 1–67' | | Q–P | |
| NE of W Middletown | Wilsons Mills | | Cross Creek | 1–35' | | Q–P | |
| N of W Middletown | Thompson | T | Cross Creek | 1–25' | | K–P | |
| N of Paris | Ralston (or Freeman) | | Aunt Clara's Fk of Kings Creek | 1–28' | | Q–P | |
| E of Florence | Lyle | | Brush Run | 1–31' | | Q–P | |
| NW of Taylortown | Saw Hill | | Buffalo Creek | 1–48' | | Q–P | |
| N of Marianna | McGuiness | T | Daniels Run | 1–39' | | Q–P | |
| S of Florence | Doc Hanlin | P | Harmon Creek | 1–22' | | K–P | By-passed |
| N of Paris | Devil's Den (or Run) | | Kings Creek | 1–24' | | K–P | |
| NE of Paris | Jackson's Mill | | Kings Creek | 1–39' | | Q–P | |
| SE of W Alexander | Mays (or Blaney) | | Br Middle Wheeling Creek | 1–31' | 1882 | Q–P | |
| S of W Alexander | Erskine | | Middle Wheeling Creek | 1–47' | 1845 | Q–P | William Gordon |
| E of Eightyfour | Henry | | Mingo Creek | 1–45' | | Q–P | |
| NW of Bentleyville | Wright | | N Fk Pigeon Creek | 1–35' | | K–P | |
| SE of Cherry Valley | Krepps | | Raccoon Creek | 1–24' | | K–P | |
| W of Twilight | Ebeneezer Church | | S Br Maple Creek | 1–32' | | Q–P | Preserved |
| E of Glyde | Leatherman | | S Fk Pigeon Creek | 1–45' | | Q–P | |

## WESTMORELAND COUNTY

| Location | Name | Owner | Stream | Spans & Length | Date | Type | Builder, etc. |
|---|---|---|---|---|---|---|---|
| E of W Newton | Bell's Mill | | Big Sewickley Creek | 1–90' | 1850 | Burr | Daniel McOain |

## YORK COUNTY

| Location | Name | Owner | Stream | Spans & Length | Date | Type | Builder, etc. |
|---|---|---|---|---|---|---|---|
| Roler | Detters Mill | | Conewago Creek | 2–258' | | Burr | |
| NW of Foustown | Bentzell's Mill | | Little Conewago Creek | 1–97' | | Burr | |

# VIRGINIA

## ALLEGHANY COUNTY

| Location | Name | Owner | Stream | Spans & Length | Date | Type | Builder, etc. |
|---|---|---|---|---|---|---|---|
| W of Covington | Humpback | T | Dunlop Creek | 1–100' | 1835 | Burr Adapt. | Venable[37] |

## CAMPBELL COUNTY

| Location | Name | Owner | Stream | Spans & Length | Date | Type | Builder, etc. |
|---|---|---|---|---|---|---|---|
| SW of Gladys | Marysville | | Seneca River | 1–60' | 1878 | | |

## GILES COUNTY

| Location | Name | Owner | Stream | Spans & Length | Date | Type | Builder, etc. |
|---|---|---|---|---|---|---|---|
| NE of Newport | Maple Shade | P | Sinking Creek | 1–36' | 1919 | Burr | |
| NW of Newport | | | Sinking Creek | 1–50' | 1912 | Burr | |
| N of Newport | | | Sinking Creek | 1–70' | 1916 | Burr | |

## HALIFAX COUNTY

| Location | Name | Owner | Stream | Spans & Length | Date | Type | Builder, etc. |
|---|---|---|---|---|---|---|---|
| E of South Boston | | | Hyco River | 1–170' | 1908 | Haupt | |

## PATRICK COUNTY

| Location | Name | Owner | Stream | Spans & Length | Date | Type | Builder, etc. |
|---|---|---|---|---|---|---|---|
| S of Woolwine | | | Smith River | 1–48' | 1916 | Q–P | |
| SE of Woolwine | | | Smith River | 1–80' | 1920 | Q–P | |

## SHENANDOAH COUNTY

| Location | Name | Owner | Stream | Spans & Length | Date | Type | Builder, etc. |
|---|---|---|---|---|---|---|---|
| S of Mt. Jackson | Meems Bottom | | N Fk of Shenandoah River | 1–191' | 1892 | Burr | F. H. Wisler |

# WEST VIRGINIA

## BARBOUR COUNTY

| Location | Name | Owner | Stream | Spans & Length | Date | Type | Builder, etc. |
|---|---|---|---|---|---|---|---|
| Philippi | | T | Tygart's Valley River | 2–203' | 1852 | Burr | Lemuel Chenoweth[38] |
| Carrollton | | | Buckhannon River | 1– | | Burr | |

## CABELL COUNTY

| Location | Name | Owner | Stream | Spans & Length | Date | Type | Builder, etc. |
|---|---|---|---|---|---|---|---|
| Near Milton | | | Mud River | 1– | | Howe | |
| S of Glenwood | | | Guyan Creek | 1– | | Howe A. | Abandoned |

## DODDRIDGE COUNTY

| Location | Name | Owner | Stream | Spans & Length | Date | Type | Builder, etc. |
|---|---|---|---|---|---|---|---|
| Center Point | | | Pike fk of McElroy Creek | 1– | | | |

[35]Or Bissell.      [36]Templeton Fork of Enslow's Fork of Wheeling Creek.      [37]Special arched chords.      [38]Two auxiliary piers added.

| LOCATION | NAME | OWN-ER | STREAM | SPANS & LENGTH | DATE | TYPE | BUILDER, ETC. |
|---|---|---|---|---|---|---|---|
| **GREENBRIER COUNTY** | | | | | | | |
| N of Alderson | | | Muddy Creek | 1– | | Q–P | |
| Near Alderson | | | Muddy Creek | 1– | | Q–P | |
| W of Lewisburg | Sink's Mill | | Milligan Creek | 1– | | Q–P | |
| **HARRISON COUNTY** | | | | | | | |
| Dola | | | Rt hand fk Ten Mile Creek | 1–64' | 1890 | Q–P | John F. Sturm |
| S of Marshville | Fletcher | | Ten Mile Creek | 1–60' | 1892 | Q–P | Solomon Swiger |
| Jarvisville | | | Ten Mile Creek | 1–40' | 1893 | Q–P | J. J. Spencer[39] |
| SE of Clarksburg | Stout Farm | | Brushy fk of Elk Creek | 1–28' | 1893 | Q–P | John Greathouse |
| SE of Clarksburg | Lang Farm | | Brushy fk of Elk Creek | 1–45' | 1885 | Q–P | Asa S. Hugill |
| SE of Clarksburg | Romine's Mill | | Gnatty Creek | 1–60' | 1888 | Q–P | George C. Blair |
| SE of Clarksburg | | | Rooting Creek | 1–30' | 1887 | Q–P | George C. Blair |
| S of Bridgeport | Law Farm | | Simpson Creek | 1–78' | 1881 | MK–P | Asa S. Hugill |
| N of Lost Creek | Jesse Kennedy | | Lost Creek | 1–50' | 1882 | Q–P | John W. Fox[40] |
| N of Wallace | Margaret | | Quaker fk of Bingamon Creek | 1–32' | 1893 | Q–P | J. J. Spencer[41] |
| **HARRISON-LEWIS COUNTIES** | | | | | | | |
| Near Kinchelo | | | Kinchelo Creek | 1–30' | 1897 | Q–P | W. H. Virgie |
| **JACKSON COUNTY** | | | | | | | |
| Odaville–Sandyville | | | Sandy Creek | | | | |
| Near Sandyville | | | Sandy Creek | 1– | | Burr | |
| Staats Mill | | | Tug Fork | | | | |
| **LEWIS COUNTY** | | | | | | | |
| Walkersville | | | West Fork River | 1– | | | |
| Jackson's Mill | | | West Fork River | 1– | | | |
| Roanoke | | | Sand Fork | | | | |
| Gaston | | | Stonecoal Creek | 1– | | Burr | |
| **MARION COUNTY** | | | | | | | |
| Granttown | | | Paw Paw Creek | 1– | | | |
| Barrackville | | T | Buffalo Creek | 1–145' | 1852 | Burr | L. & E. Chenoweth |
| **MONONGALIA COUNTY** | | | | | | | |
| Wadestown | | | W Va Fk Dunkard Creek | 1– | 1873 | K–P | Rufus Bell |
| Wadestown | | | N Fk Dunkard Creek | 1– | 1886 | K–P | Add Shriver |
| St. Cloud | | | Dunkard Creek | 1– | 1884 | | Milo Strosnider |
| Tannant School | | | Miracle Run | 1– | 1882 | | |
| Bula–Fairview | | P | Miracle Run | 1– | | ½ K–P | |
| Brookover Bridge | | | Day's Run | | | | |
| N of Laurel Run | | | Dent Run | 1– | 1889 | | W. A. Loar |
| **MONROE COUNTY** | | | | | | | |
| Nr Salt Sulphur Spr | | | Indian Creek | 1– | | Howe | |
| Near Lillydale | | | Laurel Creek | | | | |
| **POCAHONTAS COUNTY** | | | | | | | |
| Near Dunmore | | | Locust Creek | 2– | | Howe A. | |
| **PRESTON COUNTY** | | | | | | | |
| W of Erwin | Cheat River | T | Cheat River | 2–337' | 1837 | [42] | Josiah Kidwell[43] |
| **RITCHIE COUNTY** | | | | | | | |
| Near Cairo | | | N Fk Hughes River | 1– | | Burr | |
| Berea | | | S Fk Hughes River | 1– | | Burr | |
| Near Highland | | | Bond's Creek | | | | |
| Ironton | | | Three Fork Creek | | | | |
| **UPSHUR COUNTY** | | | | | | | |
| Holly Grove | | | Little Kanawha River | | | | |
| **WAYNE COUNTY** | | | | | | | |
| Cyrus | | | White's Creek | 1– | | Howe | |
| Near Pritchard | | | Elijah Creek | | | | |
| **WETZEL COUNTY** | | | | | | | |
| Near Hundred | | | Fish Creek | 1– | | Q–P | |

[39]And J. B. Wright.     [41]And J. B. Wright.     [42]Lewis Wernwag.     [43]From Wernwag plans.
[40]And Lloyd Sturm.

# Selected Bibliography

Brandt, Francis Burke, *The Wissahickon Valley*. Philadelphia, 1927.

Cooper, Theodore, *American Railroad Bridges*. New York, [1889].

Dare, Charles P., *Philadelphia, Wilmington & Baltimore R. R. Guide*. 1856.

Day, Sherman, *Historical Collections of the State of Pennsylvania*. 1843.

Harmer, Harvey W., *Covered Bridges of Harrison County, West Virginia*. Charleston, W. Va., 1956.

Haupt, Herman, *Reminiscences of General Herman Haupt*. New York, 1901.

Lewis, John Frederick, *The Redemption of the Lower Schuylkill*. Philadelphia, 1924.

McElree, W. W., *Down the Eastern and Up the Black Brandywine*. 1912.
———, *Along the Western Brandywine*. 1912.
———, *Around the Boundaries of Chester County*. 1934.

Mock, Elizabeth B., *The Architecture of Bridges*. New York, 1949.

Peale, Charles Willson, *An Essay on Building Wooden Bridges*. Philadelphia, 1797.

Pope, Thomas, *A Treatise on Bridge Architecture*. New York, 1811.

Sellers, Charles Coleman, *Charles Willson Peale*. 1947.

Singmaster, Elsie, *Pennsylvania's Susquehanna*. Harrisburg, Penna., 1950.

Summers, Festus P., *The Baltimore & Ohio in the Civil War*. New York, 1939.

Tyrrell, Henry G., *History of Bridge Engineering*. Chicago, 1911.

Unger, Frederick Fleming, *Old Bridges of Franklin County*. Mercersburg, Penna., 1941.

White, Henry Joseph, and Von Bernewitz, M. W., *The Bridges of Pittsburgh*. 1928.

Zucker, Paul, *American Bridges and Dams*. New York, 1941.

Also:

*American Heritage*, Summer, 1952. "The Battle of Philippi," by Eva Margaret Carnes.

*Bucks County Traveler*, September and October, 1956. "Bucks County's Covered Bridges."

*Covered Bridge Topics*, edited by Richard S. Allen, Eugene R. Bock and Leo Litwin. National Society for the Preservation of Covered Bridges. April, 1943–

*The Historical Review of Berks County*, October, 1947. "The Covered Bridges of Berks County," by Harry E. Mitchell, Jr.

*Papers Read before the Lancaster County Historical Society:*

Vol. XLI, No. 6. "Historic Bridge Building in Lancaster County," by Sister Mary Hildegarde Yeager. 1937.

Vol. XLVI, No. 4. "The First Columbia Bridge," by Robert H. Goodell. 1942.

Vol. LVII, No. 1. "The Second Columbia Bridge," by Robert H. Goodell. 1953.

Vol. LVII, No. 6. "The River to Be Crossed Rather than to Be Followed," by Richmond E. Myers. 1953.

*Pennsylvania History*, October, 1956. "Theodore Burr and his Bridges across the Susquehanna," by Hubertis M. Cummings.

# Glossary

ABUTMENT—The shore foundation upon which a bridge rests, usually built of stone but sometimes of bedrock, wood, iron or concrete.

ARCH—A structural curved timber, or arrangement of timbers, to support a bridge, usually used in covered bridges together with a truss. Thus a *supplemental* or *auxiliary arch* is one which assists a truss and forms an arch-truss; a *true arch* bridge is entirely dependent upon the arch for support.

BENT—An arrangement of timbers resembling a sawhorse which is placed under a bridge at right angles to the stringers, sometimes used as a temporary scaffolding in building a covered bridge. Also to support light, open approaches, weak or damaged bridges, and sometimes as a substitute for abutments or piers.

BRACE—A diagonal timber in a truss which slants toward the midpoint of the bridge.

CHORD—The top (*upper chord*) or bottom (*lower chord*) member or members of a bridge truss, usually formed by the stringers; may be a single piece or a series of long joined pieces.

COMBINATION BRIDGE—Bridge designed for both highway and railroad traffic; also, a structure made with two types of trusses or combining features of two different trusses.

COMPRESSION MEMBER—A timber or other truss member which is subjected to squeeze. Often a diagonal member, such as a brace (q.v.) or counterbrace (q.v.).

CORBEL—In covered bridges, a solid piece of wood —mainly for decoration—which projects from the portal and assists in supporting the overhanging roof. Also, on a larger scale, a solid timber at the angle of an abutment (or pier) and lower chord to lend extra support.

COUNTERBRACE—A diagonal timber in a truss which slants away from the midpoint of the bridge (opposite from brace, q.v.).

DECK TRUSS—A type of bridge where the traffic, usually railroad, uses the roof on top of the truss as a roadbed; sometimes also carries traffic inside, between the trusses.

DOUBLE-BARRELED BRIDGE—Common designation for a covered bridge with two lanes; the divider can be a third truss or structural part of the bridge, or it can be a simple partition.

FACE OF ABUTMENT—The side of the abutment toward the center of the stream.

FALSEWORK—See SCAFFOLDING.

FLOOR BEAM—Transverse beam between bottom chords of trusses on which longitudinal joists are laid.

JOIST—Timbers laid longitudinally on the floor beams of a bridge and over which the floor planking is laid.

KEY—Piece, often a wedge, inserted in a joint such as a mortise-and-tenon to tighten the connection. Sometimes called a *fid*.

LAMINATED ARCH—A series of planks bolted together to form an arc; constructed in such a manner that the boards are staggered to give extra strength.

LATERAL BRACING—An arrangement of timbers between the two top chords or between the two bottom chords of bridge trusses to keep the trusses spaced apart correctly and to insure their strength. The arrangement may be very simple, or complex.

MORTISE, (n)—Cavity made in wood to receive a tenon. (v)—To join or fasten securely by using a mortise and tenon.

PANEL—Rectangular section of truss included between two vertical posts and the chords. A *panel system* is made up of three or more panels.

PARAPETS—Low masonry stone walls on either side of the section of roadway leading directly into a bridge. Common in Pennsylvania.

PATENTED TRUSS—Any one of the truss types for which United States patents have been granted, such as Burr, Town, Long, Howe, etc., trusses.

PIER—An intermediate foundation between abutments, built in the streambed, for additional support for the bridge. May be made of stone, concrete, wood, etc.

PILE—Heavy timber, often a peeled log, sunk vertically into the streambed to provide a foundation when the bottom is unreliable. Piling can be used as a base for abutments and piers, or the bridge can be built directly upon piling.

PORTAL—General term for the entrance or exit of a covered bridge; also used to refer to the boarded section of either end under the roof.

POST—Upright or vertical timber in a bridge truss; *centerpost* is the vertical timber in the center of a truss; *endpost* is the vertical timber at either end of the truss.

RAFTER—One of a series of relatively narrow beams joined with its opposite number to form an inverted V to support the roof boards of a bridge.

SCAFFOLDING—Light, temporary wooden platforms built to assist in the erection of a bridge. Sometimes called *falsework.*

SECONDARY CHORD—Single or joined timbers lying between upper and lower chords and parallel to them, giving added strength to the truss.

SHELTER PANEL—The first panel at each end of both trusses of a panel-truss bridge, often boarded on the inside to protect the timbers from moisture blowing through the portals.

SHIP'S KNEE—A short timber bent at a right angle used inside a covered bridge between a truss and upper lateral bracing to increase rigidity. Similar to a corbel (q.v.) but heavier and not decorative. Sometimes called *knee brace.*

SIMPLE TRUSS—An elementary bridge truss, such as kingpost or queenpost; not so large or complex as the patented trusses.

SKEW-BACK—A jog or incline in the face of an abutment to receive the end of a chord or an arch.

SKEWED BRIDGE—A bridge built diagonally across a stream.

SPAN—The length of a bridge between abutments or piers. *Clear span* is the distance across a bridge having no intermediate support, and measured from the face of one abutment to the face of the other. The length usually given is for the *truss span,* i.e., the length between one endpost of the truss and the other, regardless of how far the truss may overreach the actual abutment. Bridges of more than one span are called *multi-span bridges.*

SPLICE—A method of joining timbers, especially end-to-end, by means of a scarf or other joint, sometimes with keys or wedges inserted to give additional strength and stability to the joint. A *splice-clamp* is a metal or wooden clamp designed to hold two spliced timbers together.

STRINGER (or String-Piece)—A longitudinal member of a truss which may be made up of either one single timber, in comparatively short bridges, or a series of timbers spliced end-to-end in longer bridges. Most evident in the chords (q.v.) which often go by this name.

SUSPENSION ROD (or Hanger Rod or Suspender)—Iron rod usually found in arch bridges or in connection with auxiliary arches added to older bridges; attached from arch to floor beams to aid in supporting the roadway.

TENON—A tongue shaped at the end of a timber to fit into a mortise and so form a joint.

TENSION MEMBER—Any timber or rod of a truss which is subjected to pull, or stretch.

TIE-ROD—Iron rod used as integral vertical member in some truss bridges to replace wooden posts between upper and lower chords. Bridge members could be tightened by adjusting nuts against washers on the ends of the rods. Their use marked the first step in transition from wooden bridges to bridges made entirely of iron.

TREENAILS—Wooden pins which are driven into holes of slightly smaller diameter to pin members of lattice trusses together (pronounced "trunnels").

TRESTLE—A braced framework built up from the streambed to support a bridge.

THROUGH TRUSS—A covered bridge in which traffic uses a roadway laid on the lower chords between the trusses. Most covered bridges are through trusses.

TRUSS—An arrangement of members, such as timbers, rods, etc., in a rigid form so united that they support each other plus whatever weight is put upon the whole. Covered bridge trusses, including arch-trusses, employ a triangle or a series of combined triangles. *Truss* can designate just one side of a bridge, generally is used as meaning the combined sides.

TURNBUCKLE—A metal loop fashioned with a screw at one end and a swivel at the other, used in some covered bridge trusses to tighten iron rods and thus overcome sagging.

WEB—A truss design (such as Town lattice) in which timbers crisscross each other. A lattice truss, or a truss designed with overlapping panels, may be called a *web system.*

WEDGE—See Key.

WINDBRACING—Inside timbers extending from a point on a truss to the ridgepole to attach the roof more firmly to the sides of the bridge.

# Index

Franklin, 72; Greene, 78, 79;
Huntingdon, 66; Indiana, 74;
Lancaster, 71, 72; Lawrence, 75;
Lehigh, 55, 56; Luzerne, 62;
Mercer, 74; Montgomery, 58, 59;
Northumberland, 63; Perry, 66;
Somerset, 77; Sullivan, 65;
Union, 65; Washington, 78, 79;
Westmoreland, 74; York, 70
Pennsylvania covered bridges,
    characteristics of—55, 59, 71
Pensyl's Mill (Penna.) bridge—**63**
Permanent Bridge (Philadelphia)—
    1-7, **1**, **5**, 14, 27, 57, 92
Peters, Richard—4-6, **4**
Philadelphia (Penna.) Bridges—
    1-7, 14-16, 19, 24, 27, 60-61
Philippi (W.Va.) Bridge—31, **31**,
    32, 89, 91, **91**
Phoenixville (Penna.)—16
Pine Grove (Penna.)—28
Pine Valley (Penna.) Bridge—**56**
Pittsburgh (Penna.) bridges—16,
    75, **75**, 76, **76**, 77
Pleasantville (Penna.) Bridge—58,
    **58**
Pope, Thomas—96, 97
Potomac River watershed (Penna.)
    —72, **72**
Portals—57, 60, 61, 68, **69**, 92
Porterfield, Col. George A.—31
Portland (Penna.)-Columbia
    (N.J.) Bridge—55
Preservation of bridges—79, 83, 84,
    85, 89, 91, 92, 100-104
Price and Phillips' Bridge—96, 97,

Railroads—17, 22, 24-26, 28, 30-32,
    34, 35, 39, 53, 55, 60, 61, 64,
    67, 70, 71, 94
Railroad covered bridges—16, 17-
    28, **19**, **20**, **22**, **23**, **24**, **26**, **27**,
    **28**, 29, 31, 32, 34, 35, **35**, 37,
    **38**, 39, 52, **52**, 53, **58**, 60, **60**,
    63, 64, 67, **67**, 70, **70**, 71, 94,
    **100**
Reading (Penna.) bridges—57, 58
Red Hill (Penna.) Bridge—**58**, 59
Relay (Md.)—18
Remington, John R.—97
Reynolds Bridge (Md.)—48
Richmond (Va.) railroad bridge—
    **23**, 24
Riegelsville (Penna.-N.J.)—55
Rising Sun (Del.)—41, **41**
Roebling, John A.—76
Roads—*see* Turnpikes
Roberts, William Milnor—24
Robinson, Moncure—23, **23**, 24
Robinson, Samuel—4
Rockland (Del.) Bridge—41
Rock Run (Md.) Bridge—44-46
Rockville (Penna.) Bridge—26
Roddy Bridge (Md.)—47, **49**
Rogers, Isaiah—97
Romine's Mill Bridge (W.Va.)—
    **90**, 91
Romney (W.Va.)—**32**
Rooting Creek (W.Va.) Bridge—**90**
Rush, William—6, 57
Ryot (Penna.) Bridge—**66**

S-shaped bridge—16, **19**, 29, **29**
Sabotage of covered bridges—31,

32, 35, 36, 39
Salunga (Penna.) Bridge—**71**
Sandyville (W.Va.) Bridge—**90**
Sauk's Bridge (Penna.)— 72, **72**
Schuler, Andrew—103
Schuylkill Permanent Bridge Co.—
    3, 6
Scott's Bridge (Md.)—48
Sharpsburg (Md.)—36
Sheard's Mill Bridge (Penna.)—**56**
Shearer's Mill Bridge (Penna.)—
    71, 72
Signs on bridges—1, 6, 32, 36, 56,
    60, 73, 83, 99
Sink's Mill Bridge (W.Va.)—**90**
Sitler, Harold and family—102, **102**
Slaymaker, Henry & Samuel—7, 9
Smith, Robert H.—104
Smith, Robert W.—74 —*see also*
    Truss Types
Smith's Bridge (Del.)—43, **43**
Smith's Ferry (Penna.) Railroad
    Bridge—**100**
Smith's Sawmill Bridge (Penna.)
    **104**
Smithsonian Institution—97
Snavely's Mill (Penna.) Bridge—
    72, **72**
South Boston (Va.) Bridge—81, **81**
South Perkasie (Penna.) Bridge—
    56, 103, **103**
Spring Garden (Penna.) Bridge—
    **101**
Stillwater (Penna.) Bridge—63
Stone as a bridge building material
    18, 19, 24, 46
Stone, Daniel—17, 26, 27
Stoudt's Ferry (Penna.) Bridge—
    57, 58, **58**
Summit Bridge (Del.)—41, 42, **42**
Sundale (Penna.)—**56**
Susquehanna River watershed
    (Penna.)—61-72, **62**
Sutton, David—57
Swiftwater Inn Bridge (Penna.)
    —104, **104**

Tests of covered bridges—15, 22
Thayer, George W.—52
Theodore Burr Covered Bridge
    Society of Pennsylvania—102
Thomas Mill (Philadelphia)
    Bridge—61, **61**
Thompson, Joseph—16, 75
Thompson's Bridge (Del.)—41
Toll Bridges—98
Torpedoes, use of in bridge sabo-
    tage—34, **34**, 35
Towanda (Penna.) Bridge—61
Town, Ithiel—17, 22, 23, 24, 26,
    56, 57, 80, 95 —*see also* Truss
    Types
Traquair, Adam—6
Trestle bridges—35, 36
Truss Types:
    Brown-Allen—20, 21, **21**, 25
    Burr—8, **8**
    Haupt—81, **81**
    Howe—26, **27**
    Latrobe—21, **22**
    Long—18, 74
    McCallum—25, **25**
    Smith—74, **74**

Town Lattice—22
Wernwag—14, 15, **15**, **88**
—*see also Appendix I*
Turnpikes and Great Roads:
    Buckeystown, 46; Cumberland,
    46; Frankford-Bristol, 14; Har-
    ford, 45; James River & Ka-
    nawha, 13, 83, 86; Jefferson, 46;
    Leesburg & Georgetown, 93;
    Maysville, 16; Midland Trail,
    86; National, 16, 86, 87; North-
    western, 16, 87; Pennsylvania,
    66; Staunton & Parkersburg, 88,
    89; Street, 45; Washington, 17
Twin Bridges (Penna.)—63 (and
    on book jacket)

Uhlertown (Penna.) Bridges—opp.
    table of contents—55, 57
United Daughters of the Confeder-
    acy—31
Upper Black Eddy (Penna.-N.J.)—
    55
Utica Mills (Md.) Bridge—47, **49**

Valley Forge (Penna.)—59
Vandalism—101, 102
Van Sandt's Bridge (Penna.)—**56**
Vickers, Thomas—4
Virginia, covered bridges of—80-85
Virginius (W.Va.)—16

Wadestown (W.Va.) Bridge—**90**
Wagner, Vera H.—102
Wagner's Mill (Penna.) Bridge—
    **66**
Walcott, Jonathan—7, 8, 9, 13
Wallace, Col. Lew—32
Washington, George—59, 87, 92
Wernwag, Lewis—14-16, 19, 29-31,
    41, 44, 45, 52, 53, 55, 57, 60, 61,
    75, 87, 88 —*see also* Truss Types
Westmont Station (Penna.) Bridge
    —70, **70**, 71
Weston, William—4
Weston (W.Va.)—39, 92
West Union (W.Va.) Bridge—87,
    **87**
West Virginia, covered bridges of
    —86-92
Wever, Caspar—18
Weygandt, Cornelius—100
Wheeling (W.Va.)—*see* Belmont-
    Wheeling Bridge
White, Ammi—97
Wilkes-Barre (Penna.) Bridge—12
Willey, Col. William J.—31
Williams, Wilson H.—66
Wills, George R.—102
Wilmington (Del.) Bridges—16,
    41, **41**
Winchester (Va.)—19
Wissahickon Creek (Penna.)
    bridges—**61**
Wood, as a bridge building
    material—66
Woodbine (Md.) Bridge—104
Wooddale (Del.) Bridge—**42**, 43
Woolwine (Va.) bridges—81, **81**,
    82

Y-shaped bridges—19, **19**, **26-27**,
    27, 28
Yardleyville (Penna.-N.J.) Bridge
    —23

River Buffs

624
A
Allen, Richard Sanders
Covered bridges of the
Middle Atlantic States
FEB 1

M 9296

624                    River Buffs
A                           93
Allen, Richard Sanders
Covered bridges of the Middle
Atlantic States